JESSE JAMES

JESSE JAMES

The Best Writings on the Notorious Outlaw and His Gang

EDITED BY HAROLD DELLINGER

GUILFORD, CONNECTICUT

Text design by Lisa Reneson
Cover photo: Library of Congress, LC-USZ62-3854

Library of Congress Cataloging-in-Publication Data
Jesse James : the best writings on the notorious outlaw and his gang / [edited by] Harold Dellinger. — 1st ed.
p. cm.
ISBN-13: 978-0-7627-4479-4
ISBN-10: 0-7627-4479-0
1. James, Jesse, 1847–1882. 2. James, Jesse, 1847–1882—Friends and associates. 3. James, Jesse, 1847–1882—Miscellanea. 4. Outlaws—West (U.S.)—Biography. 5. West (U.S.)—Biography. 6. Frontier and pioneer life—West (U.S.) 7. West (U.S.)—History—1860–1890. I. Dellinger, Harold.
F594.J27J47 2007
364.15'52'092—dc22

[B] 2006102059

Manufactured in the United States of America
First Edition/First Printing

The subject of greatness was being discussed as a party of us grouped around Mark Twain in a Louisville hotel lobby.

"Greatness may be classed as the ability to win recognition," said the famous humorist. "Some time ago I was making a purchase in a small town store in Missouri. A man walked in and, seeing me, came over with outstretched hand and said, 'You're Mark Twain, ain't you?'

"I nodded."

" 'Guess you and I are 'bout the greatest in our line,' he remarked. To this I couldn't nod, but I began to wonder as to what throne of greatness he held.

" 'What is your name?' I inquired.

" 'Jesse James,' he replied, gathering up his packages."

Opie Read
Mark Twain and I, 1940

. . . Outside my window about a quarter of a mile to the west there stands a little yellow house, with a green paling, and a crowd of people pulling it all down. It is the house of the great train-robber and murderer, Jesse James, who was shot by his pal last week, and the people are relic-hunters.

They sold his dust-bin and foot-scraper yesterday by public auction, his door-knocker is to be offered for sale this afternoon, the reserve price being about the income of an English bishop. The citizens of Kansas have telegraphed to an agent here to secure his coal-scuttle at all hazards and at any cost, and his favourite chromo-lithograph was disposed of at a price which in Europe only an authentic Titian can command, or an undoubted Mantegna. The Americans are certainly great hero-worshippers, and always take their heroes from the criminal classes . . .

Oscar Wilde
In a letter to Norman Forbes-Robertson
April 19, 1882

TABLE OF CONTENTS

PART II: WHO HAD KILLED MANY MEN

PART III: AND LAID POOR JESSE IN HIS GRAVE

Library of Congress, LC-USZ62-38555

A young Jesse James, shown wearing a Civil War–era guerilla shirt. This photo was taken circa 1864, when Jesse was sixteen years old.

FOREWORD

By Harold Dellinger

There is an old story (some even insist that it's true) about a poll taken in Europe. The pollsters asked innocent passersby the following question: "Who are the most famous Americans of all time, dead or alive?" The answer, in the story, is always Mark Twain, Mickey Mouse, and Jesse James, with the latter being touted as the most famous of all.

As cultural icons go, you would be hard-pressed to find one more enduring than Jesse James. He has been lionized as a hero and despised as a villain. After a career spent robbing from the rich (but seldom giving to the poor) and finally having been murdered by his very own Judas Iscariot, he has been the principal subject of more than five hundred English-language books and, as a secondary figure, has appeared in at least another thousand. This isn't even counting the newspaper articles, stage productions, movies, poems, essays, and songs. How does one explain the fascination? What is it about Jesse James that has so thoroughly captured our imagination?

It's a story that has all the elements of a classical epic, although displaced to the heartland. Courage, love, friendship, and betrayal; a handsome young Civil War soldier turned vengeful bank robber (albeit one with great style and humor); a thirty-four-year-old family man betrayed by an admirer who was himself a pawn of larger, well-monied forces; and a life and death almost immediately set to music and disseminated across the world.

Ironically, despite all the writings about Jesse James, there is scarcely a single uncontested fact about him. When the granddaughter of Jesse James, Jo Ross, exited from the premiere of Darryl Zanuck's 1939 movie, *Jesse James*, she was quoted as saying, "It may be entertainment, but it isn't Jesse James . . . about all the connection it had with fact was that there was once a man named James and he did ride a horse."

From the hundreds of thousands of pages written about Jesse James and his gang, I have tried to base the selections in this book largely on the character of Jesse himself. Contradictory, convoluted, layered, for every solid fact there are a dozen rumors and fabrications. For every champion, there's a detractor. If there are truths to be found in this complicated body of work, they are most likely in the shape of the larger whole, in the cracks between the pages. Bouncing from novel excerpts and biographies, song lyrics to modern poetry, in compiling this anthology, I've tried to pull the best pieces from a compelling and controversial bunch. I hope you enjoy reading them as much as I've enjoyed gathering them.

PART 1

JESSE JAMES WAS HIS NAME

Library of Congress, LC-USZ62-13631

The child is the father of the man, it is said. Unfortunately, when it comes to Jesse James, his childhood is perhaps the least known part of his life.

To flesh out Jesse James's beginnings, we've excerpted a portion of William Settle's masterful biography as well as a piece by Jim Cummins, a childhood friend of Jesse's, who describes what it was like to grow up on the Missouri frontier in the shadow of the Kansas–Missouri Border Wars. The violence that Jesse James and his family experienced in the early years of Jesse's life no doubt informed his later years.

A portion of John Newman Edwards's "interview" with Jesse James is herein published for the first time in book form in the United States. This is also the only known interview with Jesse James. It is here that we see developed for the first time a number of the elements that would later become part of the mythology of Jesse James.

The end of the Civil War found Jesse severely wounded, his cause defeated, and his family threatened economically and politically by Reconstruction. In retrospect, the development of an outlaw career seems almost inevitable.

— Harold Dellinger

FROM

STRENUOUS AMERICANS

By R. F. Dibble

1925

The full life of Jesse James has never been written, and it never can be. A man—a sparsely documented yet definite personality—who bore that name was, it is true, born on September 5, 1847, and died on April 3, 1882. But he left hardly a single authenticated account of himself, and the hundreds of records that were penned about him (mostly cheap-printed booklets with glaring yellow covers and crudely fictitious pictures, and newspaper items without number) have in great part disappeared. Of the few that are still extant there are two species: those of idolizing relatives and mawkish hero-worshipers, or those of malignant enemies and pseudo-reformers who keenly realized the financial opportunities that lay in inverted hagiologies—books which made crime doubly odious by painting the blackest deeds of the criminal an even deeper black, and which proved their indubitable moral worth by juxtaposing one-tenth of virtue with nine-tenths of vice. The fabulists who wrote these tales manifest a curious parallelism in the presentation of their material; a parallelism that often extends even to the position of commas and abundant exclamation points. Unquestionably, the enormous sale that their fabrications have had, and indeed still have, both at home and abroad, fully justifies the faith, as well as the business acumen, of the authors. Who can doubt that thousands of the youngsters who have been frightened into docility when parental wisdom has brandished the bogey of Jesse James over their terrified heads, or who have surreptitiously perused the bloody record of America's greatest bandit with pounding pulse, with breathless rapidity, and with horrified delight, have heeded its solemn warnings and lived virtuously ever after?

If, then, the facts about the life of this strange, shadowy individual are few, and if only those facts can be accepted as approximate truth which are attested by both his defamers and his panegyrists, even less is known concerning his personality, concerning, in a vital sense, his character. Was he a saint or a devil, a hero or a villain, a patriot or a rascal, a chivalrous knight or a dragon in human form—or was he an insoluble compound of such opposites? Was he a brave soul fighting against an inauspicious destiny, or was he a low, scoundrelly chap, courageous to be sure, but repulsive and brutal, a murderer and a cutthroat who killed just for the fun of killing? He was—and he was not. The truth is that "Jesse James" never lived at all; he was a pure creation of the mind. He was born, he lived, he died, in the complex and far-reaching imagination of his race. He was America's Odysseus, America's Beowulf, America's Robin Hood. He was the Mr. Impossibly Bad Man, the Mr. Impossibly Good Man, who has lived in every land and age. An ordinary enough fellow in his mundane life, probably, like most of us; but it was his fortune to be transformed beyond recognition into the rogue-superman, the demon-god, of his time, and to be endowed with fantastic and chimerical qualities—to be a myth and a legend while he still lived in the flesh.

This arresting, this fascinating person is, in truth, merely the embodiment of a superstitious belief. He is only an emblem, a symbolic name—but what a name! It does not appear, to be sure, among the lists of America's most important sons, it is not to be found in those respectable histories that purport to give a full account of all the forces that have touched her most deeply; and yet, from the standpoint of significantly concealed influences upon the mind of youth, and not seldom of maturity, it is certainly of much greater importance than many names which have been scholastically honored and popularly forgotten. No, our hero has not yet received his due; and the reason therefor is not far to seek. Viewed in the light of stolid, plodding, tradition-loving respectability—and the nineteenth century was sufficiently stolid, plodding, and tradition-loving—he is by no means a desirable national character. Under the circumstances, it has been thought that the most expedient thing to do was to be painstakingly oblivious of his existence, to treat him as poor relations are wont to be treated, and to push him into limbo as speedily as possible.

This has been done—only by the elect minority. But the difficulty with this commendable policy lies in the fact that the profane folk-imagination which surrounded Jesse James with a nimbus of mingled glory and odium was one of the vital elements of that century; that, even today, it still surrounds him and his spiritual bedfellows who, to the delight of the multitudes, swagger along their rascally ways in sensational fiction, in the cinema, and even in actual life. Can it be that the egregious morality of the last century preferred not to face uncomfortable facts—specifically, the fact of Jesse James? Did it hate to admit that villainy sometimes has an alluring quality that virtue does not invariably possess, that the mass of people was attracted to this man because, whether partly or wholly bad, he was human, and that it was somewhat repelled by the most eminent representatives of the time because those beings were depicted, commonly with their own approbation, as just a little too good to be quite human? Whatever the explanation may be, the fact is clear: the king of American desperadoes was a more real and lively influence upon many—no one can say how many—Americans than were the Presidents in power during the sixteen years of his domination in the realm of Western Romance. In a country that was rapidly becoming tame and civilized, he stood for everything baroque and barbaric; he was the personification of all that was wild, uncultured, savage, and opposed to the trend of the times. The New England Brahmins, in particular, did not quite see how he could fit into their transcendental scheme. He revivified the days of the first settlers, when each man went armed against the relentless aborigines who might be lurking behind every bush and tree. Jesse James! The magical words are pregnant with romance. Their terse, alliterative compactness was of heroic stuff, so the people felt. It was distinctly a name worthy of a great man, worthy of a President. In truth, it seems possible that the name may account, as much as anything, for his reputation; so far as one can see, he was not essentially greater than the others in his gang, except in this one point. His brother, Frank, appears to have equaled him in almost every way; but—*Frank* James! No, it wouldn't do; it sounded altogether too prosy and common to fit a demi-god and demi-devil. Yet the lives of these two brothers were remarkably similar—even more so than the careers of two contemporary brothers who bore the same name. Comparison may properly cease at this point, except that one cannot escape noticing how thoroughly the more notorious pair exemplified, in their chief pursuits, the gospel of pragmatism that was so vigorously expounded by one of the other brothers, although he might have feared that they were overzealous.

But it is high time for the chief actor to come forth. His manners may be a little uncouth, his language—although he speaks but rarely, preferring deeds to words—not too refined, and squeamish individuals may choose to leave before the entertainment begins. The dramatic unities are at times necessarily disregarded, and the protagonist does not stand out so sharply as would be desirable; but the vast panorama of action, and the obscuring shadows that have fallen thickly upon various points of a forty-year-old story, preclude a clear-cut and well-rounded performance. It does not profess to have any particular moral, yet it offers abundant opportunity for moralizing; and so, perhaps, after all, tender-hearted folks may not find it wholly profitless to remain.

FROM

JESSE JAMES: MY FATHER

By Jesse James Jr.

1899

My grandfather, Robert James, was a Baptist preacher of wide renown in the early days in Western Missouri. He was born and raised in Kentucky, and was a graduate of the Georgetown, Ky., college. His family was one of the old families of Logan County, Ky. My grandfather was married to my grandmother, Miss Zerelda Cole, one year before he graduated. He was then 23 years old, and she was 17. They met first at a religious gathering and it was a case of love at first sight. My grandmother's people lived in Lexington, Ky., and she was educated in a Catholic convent in that city. The Cole family, of which my grandmother was a member, was of old Revolutionary stock. Her grandfather was a soldier in the war of the Revolution. My grandmother's mother was a Lindsay, of the famous old Lindsay family of Kentucky. Senator Lindsay is a member of this family.

My grandfather and grandmother were married December 28, 1841. The following August they came to Clay County, Mo., to visit the mother of Mr. James, who had married her second husband and was living in that county. He left my grandmother in Clay County and returned to Kentucky. He was to have returned the next Christmas, but the Missouri river was frozen and he had to postpone the trip. He came in the spring. My grandfather liked Clay County and he remained there, settling near Kearney. He combined farming with preaching and was very successful at both. He acquired a large and valuable farm on which my grandmother yet lives, and from the product of this farm he supported his family, because he never asked money for preaching and the good farmers to whom he broke the bread of life gave him very little. He was a great exhorter and a fervid expounder of the Gospel. He founded the Baptist churches at New Hope and at Providence, which are yet in existence. He was a wonderful revivalist and he baptized many of the old settlers of Clay County who are yet living, and many more who are dead. I have had old men and women tell me of seeing him go into the water and baptize sixty converts at one time. At this time when my grandfather baptized sixty converts without leaving the water, my father, Jesse James, was fourteen months old, and he was held up in his mother's arms and saw the ceremony.

Years afterward, when my father had returned desperately wounded from the border wars, he was baptized not very far from the same place.

In 1851 my grandfather, the Rev. Robert James, went to California. The day he started Jesse James was four years old. He clung to my grandfather and cried and pleaded with him not to go away. This affected my grandfather very much, and he told my grandmother that if he had not already spent so much money in outfitting for the trip, and if had not promised the other men who were going with him, he would give up the trip. It was a great desire to get money to educate his children, that led him to undertake the journey to the gold fields of California. My grandmother had a presentiment then that she would never see him again, and she never did. The overland trip from Clay County to California lasted from April 12 to August 1, three months. My grandfather lived only eighteen days after reaching California, and was buried there.

He had preached the gospel for eight years and received in all that time less than $100 for his services. He was a good Christian and a noble man.

The children of my grandfather were:

Alexander James, born January 10, 1844.

Robert James, born July 19, 1845, died in infancy

Jesse W. James, born September 5, 1847, died April 3, 1882.

Susan L. James, born November 25, 1849, married November 24, 1870, to Allen H. Palmer, died 1889.

My grandmother remained a widow for four years. She married Dr. Reuben Samuels in 1855. The children born of that marriage were:

Sarah L. Samuels, born December 26, 1858, married November 28, 1878, to William Nicholson.

John T. Samuels, born May 25, 1861, married July 22, 1885, to Norma L. Maret.

Fannie Quantrell Samuels, born October 18, 1863, married December 30, 1880, to Joseph Hall.

Archie Payton Samuels, born July 26, 1866, murdered by Pinkerton detectives, January 26, 1875.

My grandmother had eight children. Two of them were murdered.

My grandmother lives yet on the old homestead near Kearney, Mo. Dr. Samuels, her second husband, lives with her, but is old and quite feeble. My grandmother is seventy-four years old, is vigorous and in good health.

FROM

THE LIFE STORY OF THE JAMES AND YOUNGER GANG AND THEIR COMRADES,

Including the Operations of Quantrell's Guerillas by One Who Rode with Them: A True but Terrible Tale of Outlawry

By Jim Cummins

1903

Away back in the thirties, or early forties, of the last century William Thomason, a maternal uncle of the "James Boys," when but a youth of sixteen or seventeen years, ran away from his father's house in the northeastern part of the county, went to the then unknown Wild West, and lived, trapped and hunted with the wild Indians of the plains and the Rocky mountains, not returning again to civilization until a matured man of some thirty years of age. He had become almost as wild as his savage associates of the hunt and the war path. Physically he was a powerful man, more than a match for any two frontiersmen. Less than six feet in his moccasins, he was sturdily built, with sinews and muscles like toughened steel. His hair was black as the raven's wing, thick and heavy as the mane of a mustang and hung below his belt. He often wore his hair inside of his belt, which, with his complete suit of Indian buckskin, highly ornamented and beaded, gave him a wild, yet fascinating appearance. He had a great reputation among the Indians and had great power and influence over them by reason of his superior sagacity, his prowess as a hunter and trapper and his fearless courage in times of peril. The early plainsmen told many stories of "Wild Bill Thomason," who was the first "Wild Bill" of that wild and woolly country. There have been many "Wild Bills" since his day, but none greater, none more honorable than this Clay county product.

He was a lover of his country, true to his government and invaluable as a scout with the Indians for the frontier army of the United States.

While hunting with a party of United States soldiers and friendly Indians, for buffalo with which to supply the troops in meat, when all ammunition had been expended, and no game taken, Bill, superbly mounted on his famous black horse, captured from a wild herd, ran alongside of a splendid bison, sprang from the back of his horse to the back of the buffalo and rode him until with repeated thrusts of his knife he killed the beast and furnished the desired ration. Bill was commissioned a lieutenant in the United States Volunteer Army for the war with Mexico, and in one of the sanguinary battles in which the American troops were greatly outnumbered, Bill, with the thin line of Americans, stormed the works of the enemy. Becoming somewhat scattered from the main force, Bill went over the breast-works into a battery of Mexican artillery and captured the whole company single handed and alone.

For gallantry and meritorious conduct on this occasion he was commended to the Secretary of War by his commanding general and honorably mentioned by that official in his report to congress. The war with Mexico having ended, Bill donned his Indian garb and returned to his trapping and hunting and his Indian friends. Not long after this we find him at his old home in Clay county, on his first visit to his parents and family, in the garb described at the beginning of this chapter. He was mild mannered, gentlemanly and courteous, with a grave respect for the good people of his old home and community. Every now and then in his lighter moods, he would regale his young friends with stories of Indian wars, bear hunts, buffalo hunts, etc., and give them specimens of Comanche riding, Indian war whoops and dances.

At this age and time camp meetings were much in vogue, and were looked forward to by the early settlers as the big time of all the year, the good people, as a glorious time of refreshing and conversion of sinners, and the wild and wicked, as a time of fun and frolic, the toughs and gamblers, as a time of gain. The most noted of these meetings was held annually at the old Shady Grove Camp Ground, about five miles south of the home of Bill's parents. Many times the toughs would try to break up these meetings and the good elders and deacons had to watch as well as pray, and sometimes had to fight a little, too, to drive off the intruders and hold the consecrated ground for the Lord's cause.

Bill was always an attendant at these meetings when in that part of the country; whether the camp and out-door life, the crowd, or the service was the attraction for him, we cannot say—but he was there, and always quiet, attentive and well behaved.

It so happened that the first time he attended this meeting the church people were having more trouble than usual, and it looked for a time like the emissaries of Satan were about to be successful in driving the good people from the ground. At the night meeting in the camp, the forces on both sides had been doubled, and the church people had succeeded in driving the enemy into the woods and brush and were working in police squads to find and arrest the intruders, but were on the eve of failure, when Bill came up and tendered his services. They were most thankfully received. Bill told the church people to be perfectly quiet. He stepped a few paces in front of them, lay flat down on the ground, put his ear to the ground Indian fashion, got up and walked through the dark and brush straight to the offending parties, and came back dragging two great big bullies—either one bigger than he—by their collars, every step or two smashing their faces together as easily as toy men, making the blood fly and sorely spoiling their beauty. He brought them up to the church people, and on their promising to leave the ground and annoy no more the good people told Bill to let them go. He hurled the one on his right hand around, gave him a good kick, and told him if he ever caught him misbehaving at meeting again he would break his neck, and then gave the one on his left hand the same treatment. There was no more trouble at that meeting. Bill became so well known as a regulator and as a terror to evil doers that on public days in town and at barbecues and elections, if it was known that Bill was on the ground there was sure to be a quiet and orderly day.

At the time of this visit to civilization, Frank and Jesse James, then boys of about seven or eight years of age, probably a little older, were much in the company of their uncle, Wild Bill Thomason. The James home was only about two miles, or a little more, from the Thomason home. Bill would take Frank with a squad of little negroes from his father's cabins, arm them with corn stalks, and drill them as soldiers. He taught them many Indian tricks. He taught Frank all the trick riding of the Comanche Indians, and to use gun, pistol and bow with equal deadly aim and dexterity of movement as any boy of their tribe. Frank never forgot any of his uncle's training, but as he grew in years he grew more proficient as a horseman and to be a deadly quick shot, especially with the pistol.

When our Civil war came on no man or boy was any better equipped than was Frank James. He could ride like a Centaur, shoot like a Carver or Buffalo Bill, and was hardened in thew and sinew as any stoic of the Sierras.

FROM

JESSE JAMES WAS HIS NAME: OR, FACT AND FICTION CONCERNING THE CAREERS OF THE NOTORIOUS JAMES BROTHERS OF MISSOURI.

By William A. Settle Jr.

1966

Actually, little is known or can be learned of Frank's and Jesse's boyhood. After they attained notoriety as bandits, the writers of the cheap paperback books spun many stories to show that their savagery as guerrillas and outlaws was inherent and had been manifested in childhood. One anonymous author declared that "of the milk of human kindness they had none," for they had "drunk in from their earliest days only bitterness and malice." They hated "with the hatred of the most remorseless cruelty." He described their pleasure in torturing dumb animals, cutting off the ears and tails of dogs and cats and removing the wings of birds, for the "pitiful cries of the dumb suffering things was a sort of music they delighted in." The same writer reported that rifles and pistols were common playthings for the James boys and that as children they became expert in their use. Such tales of the cruel and lethal sport of these youngsters were printed repeatedly.

There is no evidence to show that Frank and Jesse were any better or any worse than normal boys of their time and circumstance. However, these were crucial as well as rough times, and undoubtedly the great events that were happening on the Jameses' doorstep left their mark upon the boys. Clay County, in which the family lived, is separated from the western boundary of Missouri by only one county, Platte, which nestles in the great eastward bend of the Missouri River above Kansas City. South of Clay County and across the Missouri River lies Jackson County, on the Missouri-Kansas border and containing the towns of Kansas City and Independence. The three counties that extend south of Jackson County along the Kansas border are Cass, Bates, and Vernon, in that order. Clay County is bordered on the east by Ray County, with Richmond as its county seat, and south of Ray and across the Missouri lies Lafayette County. Liberty, the county seat of Clay County, is fifteen miles northeast of present-day downtown Kansas City, and Kearney (sometimes called Centerville), near the James farm, is twelve miles northeast of Liberty.

The western border of Missouri had, after the second decade of the century, been the frontier of settlement and the jumping-off place for travelers headed for the Spanish Southwest, California, and Oregon. To the west of Missouri lay the Territory of Kansas, occupied mainly by resettled tribes of Indians from the East and denied to land-hungry whites. The Missouri Compromise had prohibited slavery there, and on this issue organization of the territory had foundered. But in 1854 Congress opened Kansas and Nebraska to settlement and authorized the people to determine for themselves whether slavery should be permitted or prohibited in the territory.

Slaves made up only 9 percent of the population of Missouri, but three-fourths of the people had slave-state backgrounds. Most Missourians had favored opening the Kansas Territory without restriction on slavery, but even the proslavery men were satisfied with the arrangement made in 1854, under the presumption that Kansas would be slave and Nebraska free. Soon, however, the formation in the North of organizations to assist the migration of antislavery settlers to Kansas aroused proslavery Missourians to feverish opposition. If Kansas were a free state, they reasoned, slave property in western Missouri would not be safe.

All hell broke loose on the border. Newspapers along the border quickly suggested the use of force to keep Northerners out of Kansas. At Liberty, only fifteen miles from the Samuel farm, the *Democratic Platform* shouted: "Let every man that owns a Negro go to Kansas and settle and our Northern brethren will be compelled to hunt further north for a location." Kansas must be a slave state if half the citizens of Missouri had to emigrate there with musket in hand, prepared to die for the cause. "Shall we allow such cutthroats and murderers . . . to settle in the territory adjoining our own state? No! If popular opinion will not keep them back, we should see what virtue there is in favor of arms."

Missourians now crossed over into Kansas, some to reside, others to influence elections, and all to intimidate the emigrant from the North who opposed slavery. Jackson, Clay, Lafayette, and nearby counties were the marshaling points for these activities. Prominent citizens of this region and even some of Missouri's most important political leaders led the forays.

Soon the nation was hearing of "Bleeding Kansas," as the newly formed Republican party and the antislavery forces in the North propagandized events in Kansas for their own purposes. No doubt the violence was exaggerated and the issue of slavery overemphasized in contemporary and subsequent accounts of happenings along the Missouri-Kansas border from 1855 to 1860, but old John Brown was there, Missouri's "Border Ruffians" did raid into Kansas, and Kansans retaliated. Competition for land and conflict over claims probably caused as much violence as the slavery question. Political intrigue and rivalry for patronage in the new territory were involved, too. Anarchy prevailed, and crimes of violence—murder, theft, burning of homes, and other outrages—were common to the region. Never more than a small segment of Missouri's population was involved, but the years of lawlessness on the Missouri-Kansas frontier left bitter hatreds that influenced the nature of the irregular warfare that was to agitate Missouri from 1861 to 1865.

The James boys' mother was a Southerner, and she owned slaves. Her sympathies and those of her family were with the forces fighting to preserve slavery. It is likely that her young sons did indeed hang John Brown and other abolitionists in their play. Children could not have been so close to these violent events without being affected. Soon, even greater forces engulfed the James family and their contemporaries as civil war swept over the land.

FROM

JESSE JAMES: LAST REBEL OF THE CIVIL WAR

By T. J. Stiles

2002

The Clay County Savings Association was more than a bank: it was the physical embodiment of the Radicals' vision of themselves as the party of progress and industry. They were concentrated in the major centers of commerce, from St. Louis to Kansas City to county seats (though that was partly a result of being driven there during the war by bushwhackers). In Liberty, the nascent Republicans had coalesced around Edward M. Samuel, the town's most enterprising merchant for the past twenty years.

In 1863, Samuel and a group of Radical allies had purchased the assets of the Liberty branch of the Farmer's Bank of Missouri and reopened in the same building, as the Clay County Savings Association. Samuel himself had left in early 1865, driven away by rebel death threats, and he began a new life as a commission merchant in St. Louis (where he would commit suicide in 1869). But the Association continued on as a distinctly

Radical institution, staffed by Radical officials, including circuit clerk James Love, the bank's president.

As Clay County's Republicans organized their local bank, the realm of money and banking was passing through a revolution as sweeping as emancipation itself. In the decades before the guns erupted at Fort Sumter, the most important function of a typical bank was to issue notes. Normally it would build a reserve fund of gold coin, then make loans by issuing its own paper money. People paid each other with these privately printed notes, trusting that they could be redeemed at the issuing bank for gold. A well-run institution circulated paper worth no more than two or three times its holdings in coin.

That, at least, was the ideal. In reality, many firms—nicknamed "wildcat" banks—recklessly issued bills far beyond their gold reserves (if they had any at all), leading to frequent crashes. Under the best circumstances, banknotes would be discounted when accepted as payment, based on the issuing bank's reputation and distance, since both affected the likelihood that the bills could be redeemed in precious metal. "A man could not travel from one state to another," complained the *St. Louis Democrat*, "without suffering a shave from five to twenty-five per cent on his money." Counterfeiting was rampant: by 1860, an estimated five thousand varieties of fake notes circulated. With more than a thousand legitimate varieties in the marketplace, detecting the phonies was almost impossible. Herman Melville parodied the situation in his 1857 novel *The Confidence-Man*, in which he depicted a man trying to detect counterfeits with a counterfeit-detector that itself was counterfeit.

This confusing, inconsistent system crashed for the last time in 1861. As war erupted, nervous Americans rushed to return their bills for gold. At the same time, the federal government was draining specie out of banks by borrowing for the war effort. From Manhattan to rural Missouri, banks suddenly stopped redeeming their notes. "There is no such thing as gold and silver coin circulating in the country," observed Senator John Sherman. "It is stowed away." The people were left with nearly worthless banknotes, while the U.S. government could no longer sell bonds to banks to finance the war effort. One way or another, Congress had to step in. As Sherman declared, "We must have money or a fractured Government."

The federal response to the crisis changed the face of the American economy forever. First, Congress created a national paper currency, immediately nicknamed the greenback. Unlike private banknotes, the greenback was legal tender—it had to be accepted as payment in all private and public transactions (except customs duties)—and, unlike almost every other kind of paper money in American history, it could not be redeemed in gold. It was money not because it represented an underlying, intrinsically valuable commodity, but because the law said so. Next, Congress established a system of national banks with federal charters (all existing banks were either private or state-chartered). It took this step partly to stabilize the country's financial structure, partly to guarantee a market for U.S. bonds (each national bank was required to maintain a reserve of federal securities). To drive state-chartered banks into the system, it levied a lethal 10 percent tax on their notes. As a result, only national banks could afford to issue paper money—and this, too, was standardized. The new national banknotes were stamped with the issuing bank's identity, and made redeemable in greenbacks, not gold. By the end of 1865, almost a thousand state banks across the country had converted into national ones.

But, at the same time, the law created a rural niche for state and private institutions, because congressional requirements made it almost impossible to organize a national bank outside of a large city. In towns with fewer than six thousand people, a national bank had to have a minimum capital stock of $50,000—a figure that was doubled for towns of between six thousand and fifty thousand residents. This was an immense sum at the end of the Civil War, especially in war-racked Missouri. The second problem was that national banks were forbidden to make mortgage loans—and, needless to say, land was the primary asset in farm country. On both counts, then, there was plenty of room in Clay County for a private or state-chartered bank, even if it could not issue notes of its own.

What Clay County Savings Association did was buy and sell money. And in postwar Missouri, money was physical, and it was scanty. It was physical because the checking account remained a largely urban phenomenon; only in the great cities, where banks were dense and clearinghouses had been established, could it play a significant role. Rural areas depended on cash—as of October 1, 1865, only $460,844,229 in greenbacks and national banknotes were in circulation. In a nation of roughly 35 million people, that meant that only $13.17 existed per person (plus 43¢ in coin). Even this figure exaggerates the amount of money available, since a significant proportion of physical currency, along with almost all checking deposits, was concentrated in the bank-rich Northeast, especially in New York City.

The result was sometimes a staggering cash drought, as families often went for weeks at a time without any coin or currency on hand. "When I was growing up there was no such thing as money," recalled Clark Griffith, the cofounder of baseball's American League, who grew up in a cash-starved town in post–Civil War Missouri, where "the medium of exchange was apple butter." Things were never quite so grave in Clay County, a center of commercial, market-oriented agriculture. But there as elsewhere improvisation reigned. The most popular form of ad hoc currency was government securities, especially Missouri's Union Military bonds and the federal 5:20 and 7:30 bonds (the first named after its minimum and maximum terms of maturity, the second after its interest rate). But they could not simply be traded at face value due to the complications of accruing interest, paid in gold dollars, which had a much higher value, dollar for dollar, than greenbacks.

In this cash-bare economy, country banks such as the Clay County Savings Association made money available by purchasing bonds, gold, silver and old banknotes, all at a healthy discount, so they could profit by reselling them in New York through correspondent banks. They also took deposits and made loans against real estate, often for small amounts, frequently as low as $100, and for terms as brief as thirty days. Rural Missourians went to banks not only to finance large purchases of land or equipment, but simply to get ready cash for a short period.

Given the dependence on physical cash, the busy trade in bonds and other financial instruments, and the raw shortage of money, the heart of the bank was the vault. Its master was the cashier. He oversaw discounting on bonds and loans, paid out cash, and kept the keys to the vault and the safe that usually sat inside. His name would appear on the bank's letterhead, across from the president's. In the Clay County Savings Association, this important personage was, as of late 1865, the peculiarly named Greenup Bird. Unlike the owners, Bird was not active in politics, but he had long been a fixture of Clay County's public life. He had signed at least one petition against the Paw Paw militia, for example; he also had served as county clerk in the 1850s, when he had helped to administer the estate of one Robert James.

At two o'clock on February 13, 1866, exactly two weeks after the owners of the Clay County Savings Association led a mass meeting of Radicals in Liberty, Bird sat at his desk in the bank writing a letter. His son William worked at a desk to his left; apart from that, the bank was empty. Suddenly the quiet scratching of nib on paper was interrupted by the creak of the door and a gust of cold air, as two men in blue soldiers' overcoats strode in. They paused in the warm space around the stove, then one of them walked up to the counter and asked to have a ten-dollar bill changed. Young Bird stood up to attend to the task—and saw a revolver in the man's hand.

William backed toward his desk as the gunman scrambled up onto the counter and leaped down. "Also the other man, drawing his revolver, followed over the counter," Greenup Bird reported. "One presenting his revolver at Wm. Bird & the other man presenting his revolver at me, [they] told us if we made any noise they would shoot us down, demanded all the money in the bank, and [said] that they wanted it quick." William stood stunned and speechless. Infuriated, his attacker spun him around and smacked him on the back with his heavy metal revolver, snarling, "Damn you, be quick!"

The first bandit pushed William into the open vault and handed him a cotton sack, telling him to put the money into it. The young clerk knelt down in front of the safe and began to pull out bags of gold and silver coin. These were special deposits (much like modern-day safety deposit boxes). In a quirk of the marketplace created by the new greenback, gold dollars were actually worth much more than the more abundant paper currency, so consumers hoarded rather than spent or invested them. "The other robber had me in tow outside of [the] vault," Greenup Bird recalled, "and demanded the greenbacks. I pointed to a tin box on the table." The man emptied it of paper dollars and bonds, then handed them through the vault entrance to the first robber, telling him to put them in the sack "and to be in a hurry." Then they shoved the cashier and his son in the vault and closed the door.

Greenup Bird listened carefully as the two men rushed back outside. When all was quiet, he shoved the door gently; it was unlocked. He cracked it open, looked and listened, then ran to the front window. "As we were going from the vault door to the window," he wrote a few days later, "I saw several men on horseback pass the window, going east, shooting off pistols." Bird hoisted open the window and shouted out the news of the robbery. At that moment, one of the horses on the street reared on its hind legs as its rider fired, killing nineteen-year-old George Wymore, who was standing opposite the bank. Wymore may have repeated Bird's shouts before he was shot, though the *Liberty Tribune* reported that he "knew nothing of the robbery, like everyone else."

Between the pair who came in the bank and their comrades waiting on the street, perhaps thirteen men galloped down Franklin Street, firing their pistols all the way. After killing Wymore they hurt no one else, thundering east out of town.

Two large posses quickly collected in Liberty and galloped in pursuit. They followed the raiders to Mount Gilead Church near Centerville, where the bandits had stopped to divide up the loot, then tracked them to a spot on the Missouri River just opposite Sibley, the bushwhackers' favorite crossing point. There the posses lost the trail. Back in Liberty, Greenup Bird and his son tallied the losses: $58,072.64 at face value.

The raid on the Clay County Savings Association was a classic bank robbery—except there was no such thing in 1866. Criminals had frequently plundered banks, of course, but almost exclusively through fraud or late-night burglary. Indeed, this event has often been called America's first daylight bank holdup in peacetime; certainly there had never been anything like it in Liberty.

From the moment that Greenup Bird shouted the alarm, it was clear that the robbers were (as bank president James Love declared) "a band of bushwhackers." In the *Liberty Tribune*, editor Robert Miller noted the universal belief that the bandits were guerrillas. "But it makes no difference who they are, or what they claim to be," he wrote, "they should be swung up in the most summary manner."

This was a startling and revealing statement. Simply put, it was an argument against the notion that *being bushwhackers* somehow justified them in their crime, or at least entitled them to sympathy. Miller never would have made this argument if a significant part of the population was not speaking of the bandits in those terms. Miller's sentence illustrates once again the three-way split between Conservatives, rebels, and Radicals, for clearly those whom Miller was trying to convince were the secessionists. After all, the Radicals hardly needed to be persuaded that the robbers should be hanged *even if* they were bushwhackers.

With blood on the streets of Liberty, the Conservatives sided with the Republicans. The pursuit of the bandits was led by William G. Garth and John S. Thomason, former militia officers who now voted the Conservative ticket. (Thomason had been a Paw Paw commander—one who actually chased and fought guerrillas—while Garth was a leading Conservative.) The other bank in town, the Liberty Savings Association, had no Radicals or even prominent Unionists among its officers, but it quickly offered its own $2,000 reward, on top of $5,000 from the victimized bank. Editor Miller, a Conservative, called for "a thorough organization of the people . . . to enable the people at a moment's notice to pursue and kill all violators of the law." On this issue Unionists of every political stripe stood together.

The Radicals, however, saw the Liberty robbery as a sign that the smoldering hatred between themselves and the bushwhackers was flaming into open warfare. With the dawn of the new year, gunfights between angry neighbors had begun to coalesce into violence on a larger scale. Already Governor Fletcher had ordered a company of militia into service in Johnson County to suppress guerrilla activity; the company killed two bushwhackers just days before the Liberty raid.

FROM

A TERRIBLE QUINTETTE

By John Newman Edwards

1873

Jesse James, the youngest [brother], has a face as smooth and as innocent as the face of a school girl. The blue eyes, very clear and penetrating, are never at rest. His form is tall, graceful and capable of great endurance and great effort. There is always a smile on his lips, and a graceful word or a compliment for all with whom he comes in contact. Looking at his small white hands, with their long, tapering fingers, one would not imagine that with a revolver they were among the quickest and deadliest in all the West. Frank is older and taller. Jesse's face is a perfect oval—Frank's is long, wide about the forehead, square and massive about the jaws and chin, and set always in a look of fixed repose. Jesse laughs at everything—Frank at nothing at all. Jesse is light-hearted, reckless, devil-may care—Frank sober, sedate, a dangerous man always in ambush in the midst of society. Jesse knows there is a price upon his head and discusses the whys and wherefores of it—Frank knows it, too, but it chafes him sorely and arouses all the tiger that is in his heart. Neither will be taken alive. Killed—that may be. Having long ago shaken hands with life, when death does come it will come to those who, neither surprised nor disappointed, will greet him with the exclamation: "How now, old fellow."

"You're accused of a multitude of bank robberies," the correspondent said, "and I have come to you for a full history of your lives, embracing of course your connection with the guerrilla service, and a recital of some of the most important actions connected therewith. If the newspaper reports can be relied on, you are certainly two of the most wonderful men in Missouri."

Jesse complied with alacrity, breaking in upon his narrative to sweep all of the horizon possible from beneath the undergrowth, and listening ever and anon as an Indian might to catch the sound of approaching hoofs or the tramp of armed and marching men.

"During the war," he commenced, "Frank and myself served under Quantrell, Todd, Anderson and Taylor."

Many of your readers will recognize these names—all of them certainly, the names of Quantrell and Alderson [sic]. George Todd was a Jackson county man, living in Kansas City when the war broke out. At first he was a lieutenant under Quantrell, and afterwards organized a company of his own and did border service that was remarkable for its desperation even in a land of desperadoes. Taylor in turn was a lieutenant under Todd, and afterwards he, too, organized a company and exhibited all the enterprise and daring of his famous leaders. Of this terrible quartette, Taylor alone survives. One of his arms was shot away in a desperate combat. The sight of one eye was for a long time endangered by another wound; for months he lay at the point of death with a bullet through his right lung, he was wounded in the left thigh and through his remaining arm, but he still survives a maimed, reticent, quiet citizen, making no moan over the past and well content that he got back from the strife with even as much of his frame as was left to him. Quantrell was killed in Kentucky, Anderson in Ray county, and Todd, while leading a forlorn charge in the Price Raid of 1864, upon the rear of the Second Colorado cavalry. The heavy ball from a Spencer rifle struck him fair in the throat, severed the jugular vein, and the man was dead almost before he touched the ground.

Jesse continued:

"Under some one of these four men we served during the war. On the 15th of May, 1865, I was wounded near Lexington, Mo., in a fight with some Wisconsin cavalry men—soldiers, I believe, of the Second Wisconsin. On the 21st of the same month I surrendered at Lexington. I was in a dreadful fix. A minie ball had gone through my right lung and everybody thought the wound would be mortal. The militia were clamoring for the death of all guerrillas, and people were afraid to come near me or about me. A Mr. Boosman, however, generously and fearlessly came to my relief, borrowed a carriage from Mrs. Early and hauled me into Lexington. On the 13th of June, 1865, I went to Kansas City, where at my uncle's in Harlem, just across the river, Dr. Johnson Lykins, a Christian if there ever was one in this world, visited me daily and did everything for my wound possible. So also did Dr. Jo. Wood, one of the noblest and best men God ever created. You see I am very particular about these things, for I want first to get at the bank robberies and murders with which Frank and myself are charged. On the 15th of July, 1865, I went up the river to Rulo, in Nebraska, were my family were. On the 26th of August I returned towards home again, but such was the condition of my wound that I was unable to be hauled to my mother's house in Clay county. Again I stopped at Harlem, at the house of my uncle, and it was here that I received the visits of Dr. Wood.

"Just able barely to mount a horse and ride about a little in the spring of 1866, my life was threatened daily, and I was forced to go heavily armed. The whole country was then full of militia, robbing, plundering and killing. As for Frank, he was never permitted to come home at all. True, he did come, but it was in defiance of the orders of the authorities and at his own peril. After remaining at home while he went to Nelson county, Kentucky, and while at Brandenburgh, got into a fight with four Federal soldiers. Two of these he killed, the third he wounded badly, and the fourth shot Frank in the point of the left hip, inflicting a terrible wound. This was in June, 1866. Frank wrote for me to come to him at once, and although my own wound was still very bad, I started immediately and stayed with him at the house of Mr. Alexander Severe, in Nelson county, until he recovered, which was in September. From Nelson county we went to Logan county to see some relatives we had there, and after staying until the middle of October, I returned alone to my home in Missouri. During the winter of 1866 and '67 I came almost to death's door. My wound would not heal, and I had several hemorrhages.

"On the night of February 18th, 1867, an effort was made to kill me. Five militia men, well armed and mounted, came to my mother's house and demanded admittance. The weather was dreadfully cold and I was in bed, scarcely able to get up. My pistols, however, I always kept by me. My step-father heard them as they walked upon the front porch and asked them what they wanted. They told him to open the door. He came to my room up stairs and asked me what he should do. I requested him to help me to the window that I might look out. He did so. There was snow on the ground and the moon was shining. I saw that the horses hitched to the fence all had cavalry saddles, and then I knew that the men were soldiers. I had but one thing to do—to drive them away or die. Surrender had played out for good for me. Incensed at my step-father's absence, they were hammering at the door with the butts of their muskets, and calling out for me to come down, swearing that they knew I was in the house and would have me out dead or alive. I went down stairs softly, got close up to the front door and listened until from the talk of the men I thought I might be able to get a pretty good range. Then putting my pistol up to within about three inches of the upper panel, I fired. One hollowed and fell. Before the surprise was off, I threw the door wide open and with a pistol in each hand began a rapid fusillade. One I killed as he ran, two more were wounded besides the one on the porch, and the fifth man got clear without a scratch. So complete was the surprise that not a man among the whole five fired a shot."

This night attack, just as it is here recorded, actually took place, the circumstances being vouched for by a large number of people in Clay county, who were quite familiar with them.

"The four wounded men were brought into my mother's house, my step-father went for a doctor, and they all recovered in a short time. Three of them are living in Clay county to-day, and are as good friends for Frank and myself have anywhere.

"I knew, however, that the next morning after the fight I would have to get away, and I did just in time, for a full company came early to look for me and were furious because I had escaped them.

"Being recommended to consult the celebrated Confederate surgeon, Dr. Paul Eve, of Nashville, Tennessee, I went there in June, 1867, and remained under his care for three weeks. He told me that my lung was so badly decayed that I was bound to die, and that the best thing I could do was to go home and die among my people. I had hope, however. I had been wounded seven times during the war, and once before in this same lung; and I did not believe I was going to die. I went from Nashville, Tennessee, to Logan county, Kentucky, and remained with my relatives until the first of November, 1867—when I again returned to Missouri. In December, I went back to Kentucky, and remained in Logan county until the latter part of January, 1868, and then went to Chaplin, Nelson county.

"About the bank robberies, Jesse," your correspondent asked, "tell me about them. According to the newspapers you and Frank have now about money enough to start a newspaper yourself, or take a goodly pile of stock in the Northern Pacific railroad."

"It was to get at the question of these robberies," Jesse replied "that has caused me to be so minute in introducing my career since the close of the war. The first robbery with which our names have been connected was the robbery of the bank at Russellville, Kentucky, which took place on March 20th, 1868. Russellville is in Logan county, and when the bank was robbed on the 20th of March, Frank and myself were at the Marshall

Hotel in Claplin, Nelson county. Should occasion ever require proof on this point, we could bring two hundred respectable people to swear that on the day of the robbery we were fifty miles from the town of Russellville. About the first of April, after suffering dreadfully from my wound, I came back to Missouri, leaving Frank behind. It was not safe for him to come to Clay county, and he did not always want to be killing.

"In May, 1868, being recommended by Dr. Joe Wood, of Kansas City, to take a sea voyage, I went to New York city to find a ship going to San Francisco. The Santiago de Cuba sailed on the 8th of June and I took passage in her. On board was a regular officer of the U.S. Army with whom I became well acquainted. Major Gregg was a noble specimen of the old-time American army officer—at that time when they had gentlemen in the army, and not shysters, Negroes, and Yankee dead-beats whom the settlers did not trust and who did not pay their gambling debts. I went with Major Gregg to Gen. Halleck's headquarters, met the General there, and had a long conversation with him concerning the nature of guerrilla warfare as practiced along the border between Missouri and Kansas. Halleck appearing to be much interested in the reminiscences I gave him of QUANTRELL, TODD, ANDERSON, BLUNT, POOL, and the rest. He proferred me assistance in any manner and advised me to leave the seacoast with my wound. I did so at once, going to the house of my uncle, D. W. James, who owned the Paso Roble Hot Sulphur Springs, San Luis Obispo county, California. These waters cured me in three weeks as if by a miracle. My wound healed, my lung got sound and strong, and from that day to this I have never felt any inconvenience from it in any manner.

"I was back again at home in Missouri, on the 28th of October, and went to work in good faith and with bright hopes for the future. Threats were made against me, however. The militia still swore that Frank should not come home, and that I should not remain there. What was I to do? Would you believe it, I plowed day in and day out with three pistols strapped about me. Around some of our fields I might have been shot from the bush, helpless and unable to defend myself.

"While working quietly at home, in December, 1869, Frank and myself were accused of robbing the bank in Gallatin, Daviess county, Missouri, and of killing at the same time its cashier, Capt. John W. Sheets. Knowing our innocence, and feeling justly indignant at a charge so infamous and untrue, Frank and myself saddled our horses, took what arms we needed to protect ourselves from our enemies and rode boldly into Kearney. Our purpose was to get affidavits from men whom the whole county knew to be truthful, and who would testify as to our whereabouts on the day of the robbery. We did get these affidavits. They were published in the columns of the Kansas City Times, a paper that has never been afraid to speak its mind on any subject, and to say a kind word even for a dog if he deserves it. These affidavits, sworn to by men of unimpeachable veracity, declared that both Frank and myself were in the town of Kearney, at 8 o'clock on the night preceding the morning of the robbery, and that we were in several stores and bought goods from several merchants. From Kearney to Gallatin is eighty miles. The robbery was committed on the 16th of December, 1869, and on the 15th of December, at 8 o'clock in the evening, both Frank and myself were buying goods in Kearney, eighty miles from Gallatin. These facts were proved by half a dozen of the best men of Clay county. Fifty more affidavits could have been procured on the same point if they had been deemed necessary. But this is not all. The night of the 16th we were again in Kearney, and again talked to a dozen or more of its citizens. To have killed Sheets and robbed the bank, and to have been in Kearney both on the nights of the 15th and 16th, it was necessary that we should have ridden one hundred and sixty miles in thirty hours on horseback. At the time we published these affidavits, I wrote a letter to Gov. McClurg, then the Governor of Missouri, pledging ourselves to surrender immediately to the officers of the law if he would protect us from a Daviess county mob—a county full of the militia the commands to which we had belonged had invariably routed. Governor McClurg did not answer my letter, but he did say, after carefully reading the evidence, that both Frank and myself were innocent of the Gallatin bank robbery.

"If the Governor had given us protection we would have gone to Gallatin cheerfully and proved to the State that we had been lied upon and slandered; but he made no motion towards it, and we were too young and too brave to be first caught and then killed as rats are killed in a trap.

"Soon after the robbery, however, the deputy sheriff of Clay county, Mr. Thomason, came to arrest me with four men. It was snowing hard at the time, and I did not recognize any of them at first. I dreaded a mob, and I had long ago made up my mind never to be taken alive. Frank and myself were soon mounted and coming to close quarters with the posse. They did not stand worth a cent. I killed Thomason's horse, and it was not until then that I knew who composed the attacking party. We rode away after the posse fled, not caring even to pursue them, much less to make a circuit, as we might have done, ambushing and killing them every one. Without one single particle of evidence to connect us with the robbery—with an abundance of undisputable testimony in our favour—the attack upon the bank was laid at our door and we were held responsible for it. Governor McClurg, however, refused to offer any reward, so convinced was he of our entire innocence in the matter."

This interview was had before the reward of $2,000 had been offered for the arrest of each by Gov. Woodson, although they knew at the time that Daviess county had offered two hundred dollars for their arrest, and the widow of Capt. Sheets four hundred more.

"But, Jesse," your correspondent proceeded, "have neither you nor Frank an idea of this Gallatin matter? Why should Sheets have been killed, who made no objection to giving up his money?"

"Yes, we have an idea of the whole thing, and a pretty clear one at that. I will tell you why Sheets was killed.

"In Bill Anderson's command there were probably fifty men who had formed what was known as the Brotherhood of Death. To become a member of it one had to swear that he would avenge the killing of a brother no matter how killed, or when, or where. Each member had a companion-in-arms, upon whom the pact became especially binding, and who could make it much more easy of observance. When Bill

Anderson was killed a captain by the name of Cox, a militia captain, boasted openly and persistently of having shot him. He showed the revolver that fired the fatal ball. He came upon the body after life was extinct and carried it into Richmond, Ray county, where a photographer could be found. Many pictures were taken of the dead lion, with his great mane of a beard, and that indescribable pallor of death on his bronzed face. One of these pictures can be seen yet, I am told, in the State Arsenal, at Jefferson City. Cox, however, did not kill Bill Anderson, although he says he did. A line of infantry, a brigade strong, was drawn up across a road Anderson was travelling to reach the Missouri River. He was a man who rode over things in preference to riding round them. He ordered a charge as soon as he struck the skirmishers and dashed ahead as he always did—the foremost rider in a band that had devils for riders. The ball that killed him was a Minie ball—Cox had only his revolver—but it was something for a militiaman to have killed the savage tiger of all the bushwhackers, and so he boasted of it, and paraded his pictures everywhere as an Indian might his scalps. Some of the Brotherhood survived the war, not many, it is true, but enough to make good the oath they had sworn. Two or three declared to me that they meant to kill Cox, if he could be got at high or low, and as Cox is said to have been a bold man they thought they would have no difficulty in finding him. I am satisfied Sheets was killed through a mistake. I am almost convinced that one of the Brotherhood did it, and that he thought he was killing Cox. At any rate Cox himself thought so, for in a very short time he sold out his property in Gallatin and removed immediately to California. This is all I can tell you of Sheets and the robbery business.

"In August, 1870, Frank and myself went to Texas, and well down upon the frontier, where we remained until the winter of 1871. With a man by the name of D. C. Wells, we visited the Indian Nation, spending some time among the Choctaws and Chickasaws. One day, I think it was on the 22d of February, and about seven miles south of Perryville, in the Creek Nation, Wells, Frank and myself met Deputy Sheriff Thomason and five men, face to face—our old antagonist of the Clay county battle. They were all well armed and so were we. A fight was expected on our side, but as they made no hostile movement, we certainly did not, and so after a little parley it was proposed that we should all dine together. Two hours were spent in this way quite pleasantly. Each party was ever on guard, but while each kept strict watch and ward, not a word was spoken that indicated in the least either vigilance or suspicion. Indeed, the deputy sheriff was greatly in need of money, and it gave me great pleasure to loan him fifty dollars, which I did then and there.

"In April, 1871, I came home again, well knowing, however, the hazard of the proceeding. On the 3d of June, 1871, a bank was robbed in Corydon, Iowa, and straightway the crime was charged upon Frank and myself. Again it was the James Boys who had done it—and again was a great hue and cry raised over our daring recklessness."

"But where were you on the third, you and Frank?"

"Frank was home in bed with a severe attack of intermittent fever, and I was in West Kansas City, at the house of Mr. Lee B. McMurtry. Mr. McMurtry was living then in the same house with Policeman McKnight, of the patrol force. I conversed freely with these two gentlemen, and with many others about the depots in the bottom. Also with a reporter from the Times by the name of Timlin. On the 5th of June a pursuing party from Corydon overtook the robbers in Daviess county and had a fight with them. The robbers whipped the Iowa men and drove them back. The day of this fight I was at home, as I can prove by three of our neighbors who were over to see us, leaving at sundown for the house of Mr. Allen Moberly, in Greenville, Clay county, where I remained until about 12 o'clock.

"On the 28th of April, 1872, the bank at Columbia, Kentucky, was robbed and the cashier killed.

"Again it was declared that Frank and myself had a hand in this robbery, and that we were not only bullet proof but ubiquitous as well. I understand, however, where most of these charges against us came from. Detective Blythe [Bligh], of Louisville, had an especial hatred against us, and for very good reasons. Whenever he could hear of a robbery that was somewhat remarkable for its boldness and its bravado, he would telegraph all over the country that the James Boys had a hand in it. He has written long letters to Major C. C. Rainwater, of the St. Louis Board of Police Commissioners, filled with his bare-faced and unscrupulous lies. Once in a fight with him our command whipped his to death, and he has never forgiven Frank and myself for the part we took in it. We know Major Rainwater well, although he does not know us. He was a gallant Confederate officer, and one who will do his duty under all circumstances. He is respected by all brave men, and I do not believe he was ever imposed on by Blythe's sensational letters and dispatches. At the time the bank was robbed in Columbia, I was in Lafayette county, Missouri. It was just after the mob in Cass county had stopped the train at Gun Town, and had killed Cline, Stevenson and Detro. Gen. Jo. O. Shelby was on the train at the time, and Frank and myself rode over to his place to learn from him the particulars of the massacre. We found him at his barn and had a long talk with him in the presence of several of his workmen. These will testify to our whereabouts.

"Again in November of the same year, I was in Lafayette county. A Negro boy at work for Gen. Shelby had been over in Aullville, had got into a fight with a white boy, and had shot at him. A mob arose and pursued the Negro with the purpose of hanging him. They had a rope along ready for his neck. I galloped down to them and bade them halt, getting between the boy and his pursuers. Covering the leader with a double-barrelled shot gun, I made the first and the last speech of my life. I told the mob that I was an outlaw myself, and that I had been driven away from home with a price upon my head. I knew nothing of the case, I said, but I was determined to resist the execution of mob-law in every shape, and that the first man who made a step further in pursuit would be certainly killed. Nobody moved, and I saved the Negro. Afterwards he was tried fairly, and acquitted.

"It takes me some time to tell you all about these bank robberies, but if you want a full confession, I propose to give it to you. The attack on the bank at Ste. Genevieve, Missouri, took place, I believe, about the 26th of May, 1873. Frank and myself were accused of being there, of course. No matter where a bank is robbed, there we are in the midst of those who suffer. Now, if Governor Woodson, to-day would pledge his official honor to protect me from the savages of a cowardly mob, I would go at once to Jefferson City and stand trial for every crime I have been charged with. So, also would Frank. When the Ste. Genevieve bank was robbed, we were in Lafayette county. I could bring as witnesses to prove my whereabouts on the 25th of May, the day preceding the robbery, twenty citizens of that county whose oaths would be taken in the court of Heaven. They saw me, talked to me, and would remember perfectly the circumstances of my meeting with each of them.

"I now come down to the Iowa train robbery, which occurred on the 21st of July, 1873, and which filled all Western Missouri with spies, detectives, and armed men in search of us. The newspapers made me out the leader of the band. With me, according to reports, were Frank James, Arthur McCoy, and the two Youngers. You remember the outlines of the robbery. A rail was removed from the track, a train thrown off, an engineer killed, and a general rifling had of an express car, thought to contain money belonging to the United States. An Iowa Sheriff named Bringhoff came down to Kansas City with a pocket full of requisitions. He made some magnificent promises—not a few threats—hunted everywhere except in the right place, and, as far as I am informed, is still in Kansas City waiting for something to turn up.

"If we were ravenous animals, we could not have been more bitterly, more unreasonably, and more savagely abused and denounced. The lying reports of the cowardly and baffled detective Blythe had been taken as gospel truth, and public sentiment, without stopping a moment to reason or to analyze, clamoured viciously for our summary arrest and punishment. The Radical papers of the State declared with emphasis that there was an organized band of robbers in Western Missouri, and that especially in Jackson county, had various members of the band been harboured and protected. Since the Iowa train robbery, however, I have not been in Jackson county, and of the day of the robbery, I had a long interview with a prominent county official, whose name I do not propose to give, even to a correspondent of the DISPATCH, a paper for which I have so much regard. I remained with him about five hours, and during that time I saw and talked with seven men who will swear that I was not in Iowa the day the attack was made upon the train.

"When it is safe for Frank and myself to surrender to the authorities of Missouri, we will do so openly and cheerfully. But it is not safe now, and so we do not mean to surrender. We may be killed, very well. It is a long lane that never has a turn. I have been shot seven times, and Frank five. Perhaps we have done a little shooting ourselves in all these years, but of that it does not become me to speak. Ask of my comrades in Jackson county, should you go back through Kansas City, what kind of soldiers we made. The best judge of a soldier on earth, is another soldier. Some of them are very hard to please, it may be, and have besides a very high standard, but when one soldier says that another soldier will fight, put it down always as gospel, that he will fight. I propose to be judged by the verdict of those with whom I served. I do not boast. In all I have said to you, I have confined myself to the God's truth, and I have tried to be brief. Should you print it, please print it as near my own way of saying it as possible."

FROM

REBEL GUN

By Arthur Steur

1956

After an hour's ride, the horsemen pulled up at a fording place in the river. The party was being led by the man on the black horse who had creased the heads of the marshals with his pistol butt. He urged his horse into the river, and the black neck of the animal frothed white. Half way across the horse had not stepped in far enough to fill the man's boots with water. The man signaled the others to follow. They crossed easily and drew up in a grove of trees on the other side. Drum dismounted and stretched his legs. Earle Younger jumped down beside him and patted him on the back.

"This is Drum Carpenter, Cole," Earle said to the man on the black horse. "This is my brother, Cole. And this is another Younger, Jim." He indicated the other rifleman who sat his horse and nodded. "And this is Payne Jones." He pointed to the man who had picked Drum from the ground and ridden before him on the saddle.

"Howdy," Payne Jones said.

"Much obliged," Drum said.

"What were you doing without your iron?" Cole Younger said. He eased himself off his horse, patting the animal to quiet him.

"I lost it. In the river," Drum said.

"Cole, wait'll you see him," Earle Younger said. He rubbed his chin where several days' stubble grew wild.

"You're lucky we lit after you," Payne Jones said.

"How did you know where I was?" Drum said.

"We tracked you," Jim Younger said. He swung one leg over the saddle and sat sideways.

"We each took a bank, two to a side, and followed downstream till we found your trail," Earle added.

"But," Drum asked, "how did you know it was my trail when you found it?" Cole Younger reached into his saddle bag and produced the belt and holster that had been dropped on the shore.

"Here," he flipped it to Drum. "Better get the buckle fixed. It falls off too easy." Earle Younger was unstrapping the bags on the horse he had taken from the dead man in Calloway's yard. He took a gun from it, checked the chambers, and handed it, butt forward to Drum. Cole Younger watched Drum put the belt on and the gun into the holster. He watched through squinted eyes, carefully. He thought he noted a look of enthusiasm. "Check that buckle," he said. Drum hesitated while he himself inspected Cole Younger. The thin-eyed man was humorless. He stood relaxed, leaning against his horse, waiting for Drum to obey. Drum nodded and fitted the buckle a notch tighter around his hips.

"You can't take it off any more," Cole Younger said, fitting his foot into his stirrup. He swung himself up and the black horse began to step as soon as he felt the weight on his back. Cole held one rein in tight and kept the animal champing in a tight circle. "Even if you do, they'll shoot you as soon as if you had it on. Then they'll testify to it. Keep it till someone takes it off and hangs it up in a saloon somewhere. Then it won't matter 'cause you won't know about it."

Cole released the reins slightly and the horse led off at a walk. Earle Younger mounted and motioned to Drum. "Ride with me, now," he said. "Give Payne's horse a rest." He took his foot from the stirrup to make room for Drum's. Drum swung up and the horsemen followed Cole Younger at a trot.

They rode until past noon, stopping only for Drum to dismount and change horses every hour or so. Then just after the sun had reached its azimuth, the country began to change. The dirt and grass gave way to rocks, smoothed round by the water shed to the Missouri, and the land sloped upward. Cole led a path through the rocks, past canyon cuts and through passages so narrow it was necessary to ride single file. Then the party pulled up before a sheer rock cliff some twenty feet high. To one side of the cliff a treacherous path led upward at a sharp angle. They waited at the wall for several minutes. Then a head appeared over the edge.

"Cole?" the voice said.

"Right," Cole Younger replied. Then, having ensured his passage, Cole spurred his horse up the trail. The animal charged the path as if it were a hurdle, surging upward in two or three strides and then disappearing over the other side to what was apparently a plateau. Each rider waited his turn, and Drum dismounted from Jim Younger's horse to lessen the weight. After all had ridden up the cliff, Drum scrambled up on foot. The plateau was a little treeless shelf in the mountain not a hundred yards square. A cabin had its back to the mountain face and was built from rough logs which must have been dropped from above or hauled over the approach which the horses had made.

Drum followed the others inside.

There were several men playing cards at a rock table on one side of the room. Another was stirring a pot of stew or soup over the open fire. The fireplace had been cut in the side of the cliff with the flue leading to a cave behind the house where the horses, supplies, and some of the men were placed. The flue was sometimes faulty, depending on the drafts in the cave, but it was also not visible from below.

Library of Congress, LC-USZ62-50007

Smith & Wesson .45 caliber Schofield said to have belonged to Jesse James.

Earle Younger introduced Drum to the others in the room: John Ross, Frank James, Bud Pence, Fetch Taylor, and Pence's brother, Don, who was in charge of the stewpot. All of them nodded, several extended their hands, but none stood up. Earle led Drum into the cabin's other room. It had a line of rough beds, covered with Union blankets over straw mattresses. On one of the beds a young man was asleep. Earle told him it was Frank James's brother, sick with fever.

They went through a door at the back of the bunk room into the cave. The dank, smoky odor was oppressive at the entrance where the ceiling was low, but farther on the cave opened into a sizeable chamber with towering height and the smoke sought the peak, leaving the air clear. Earle showed Drum the horses, the saddles, guns, ammunition, tinned goods, dried meat, beans and flour.

In the cave another card game was in progress. Drum was introduced to George Shepherd, Arch Clements, Dick Liddle, and Bill Hulse.

While they watched the game, Cole Younger came in and showed Drum a bed in the cave. He gave him a blanket, a candle, an army mess kit, and a Winchester. Then Drum followed him to the stalls and he pointed out two horses, a sprightly roan mare and a long-legged chestnut with a flowing tail. He showed Drum the feed stores, the water hole, which was an underground spring at the back of the cave, and the saddles and bridles. The two horses were put into his care, and Cole left him to his work. Drum cleaned the stalls, curried the manes and tails, and checked the teeth and hoofs. Then he carted feed and water to the horses and changed the hay. He had barely finished when dinner was called. They ate at a common table made from split logs braced on the rock tables at either end of the room. Each took his turn in line at the kettle, holding his mess kit, then returning with his tin cup for coffee. There was a mountain of doughy bread in the center of the table, but no butter and no sugar.

At the table, talk began to center around the newcomer, beginning with an account by Payne Jones of the encounter with the marshal in Usher and Drum's escape from the law. There was a great deal of amusement at the expense of the marshal and the deputy and speculation as to the state of their aching heads at the very moment.

"I don't like the idea of riding into Kansas on a fly-by-night and stirring up the redlegs," Frank James said, taking the edge off the laughter.

"Who says it was a fly-by-night?" Cole Younger answered. He scrubbed his plate with a wad of bread.

"I heard it told," Frank James said, "and that's what it sounded like to me." Frank James broke his bread in pieces and dropped them into the gravy.

"You have a right to your opinion," Cole Younger said.

"Just thought I'd try it out," Frank James said. "In general I say we ought to mind our own business unless we mean business."

"Earle spoke for the boy," Cole said. Drum kept his eyes on his plate. He could feel several pairs of eyes on him.

"I rode with him all the way up from Martinsville County," Earle said. "He broke jail to come with us. I didn't see the sense in his stewing in another one."

Jim Younger pushed his plate away from him and stood up. He took his cup and refilled it at the fire. "Earle tells us the boy is a gun hand," Jim said.

"Is that right?" Bill Hulse said. Hulse who fancied himself a superior draw, leaned over from his seat at a far corner of the table and grinned at Drum. Hulse was missing four teeth from the front of his mouth, two from the top and two from the bottom.

"Who have you fought, kid?" George Shepherd said. Shepherd had a deep bass voice and immense shoulders. He had blond hair, uncut, that hung to the shoulders. He appeared to be a gentle though powerful man. Drum looked at Shepherd and knew he had to answer. They were all silent and waiting.

"I've just been lucky," Drum said.

"Well, who have you been lucky with?" Bill Hulse asked. Drum hesitated. Something prevented him from disinterring the spirit of Forest Westram for the pleasure of that company.

"Forest Westram for one," Earle Younger interrupted, "You know him?"

"From St. Louis," Dick Liddle said. Liddle was a dandy. He brushed his hair with a shiny pomade and wore a string tie outside his collar instead of a neckerchief beneath. "He was good in his day. How old was he when they met?"

"Earle didn't see the fight," Cole Younger said. "He just heard about it."

"He was in his fifties," Drum said. "But he was still full of spring." This was the first thing Drum had said that was close to being just right.

In the opinion of Payne Jones and Donnie Pence at the far end of the table, it contained the right amount of pride without being bragging. They nodded to each other.

"He was still good from what I heard in Martinsville," Earle Younger said. "In fact they jailed the kid on the strength of his draw. They didn't believe the kid beat him."

"Why *did* he draw on you, kid?" Bill Hulse asked.

"I don't know," Drum said. "I didn't have time to ask him." The table erupted into laughter. Bud Pence, sitting next to Drum, slapped him hard on the back. The dinner began to break up as several of the men stood and moved toward the door to smoke outside.

"He's as good as I've ever seen," Earle Younger said to two or three men who still sat at the table. Drum took his plate and silver and moved away toward the cave to wash them in the spring. He could hear Earle describing the skirmish in Calloway's yard as he closed the door behind him and passed through the bunk room, head down.

"Hey," a voice said to him from the semi-darkness. Drum was startled. He tensed, and his hand moved as if to draw.

"Easy, don't shoot a sick man," the voice said. Drum relaxed, embarrassed. The voice came from one of the beds. "Is dinner over?" the voice said again.

"Yes," Drum said. "I'm sorry, you startled me."

"I'll be more careful next time." The man on the bed eased himself to a sitting position. Drum could see now that he was more his age than any of the other men. His face was smooth except for a soft thin shadow on his upper lip. "I wonder if you'd tell my brother Frank I'm hungry. I think I could eat something tonight."

"Sure," Drum said. He remembered now that the man had been pointed out to him as Frank James's brother. He went back into the main room and told Frank that his brother was awake and hungry. Frank thanked him and went to the stewpot. Drum went back out with his mess kit. "He's getting you something," Drum said.

"What's your name, jitters?" the sick man asked.

"Drum Carpenter," he answered, pretending not to notice the insult.

"Have I heard of you?"

"I don't think so," Drum said. "I just got here today."

"From the moon?" Even in the half dark Drum could see a self-satisfied smile.

"From down south, Martinsville," Drum said.

"You never heard of me, down there?"

"Should I have?"

"It would have been healthier," Jesse James said. "You maybe wouldn't have reached like you did. Don't do it when I'm standing up."

"I was surprised," Drum answered the man he still thought of merely as Frank James's sick brother. "I didn't know you were here."

"Even surprised, I wouldn't do it again, if I were you."

Drum was beginning to be irked by the man. "I said I was sorry."

"You could have been a lot sorrier," Jesse said. "You have to learn to control yourself."

"Maybe you should learn not to startle *me*," Drum said and turned his back on Jesse James to go into the cave.

He washed his mess kit and checked on the two horses. Then he went to his bed. He removed his boots for the first time in six nights. He sat on the edge of his bed and stretched his toes as he cleaned his gun, loaded it and tucked it under his pillow. Stripped except for his shirt, he crawled under the blanket. The cave was full of hollow sounds and he lay awake, thinking, wondering. Where was Quantrill? His army without its general was more like a crew of thieves. Maybe he was meeting with other generals, Lee, Sheridan, Jackson, mapping out the campaigns.

Where were his mother and Madge right now? Were they well, safe? Did they still believe in him? If only he could have spoken to them, explained how he thought.

And Julia Calloway? Alone now. What did *she* think of him? What would she have thought of him if her father were still alive? For a moment they had touched, not just their hands, but some inside part of them had met and intertwined.

He forced his brain to concentrate on the here and now, the reality of his body here in a cave on a pallet bed, a gun making a hard lump in his pillow. He closed his eyes and tried to remember the faces and names of the men he had just met; tried to put each one into his proper pocket: those who were friendly, those who resented him, and the young man who had baited him, Frank James's brother. Why had he threatened him? Was it just the fever? No, Drum thought, he was the kind who would find some kind of sore and scratch it until it bled.

FROM

THE JESSE JAMES POEMS

By Paulette Jiles

1988

Folk Tale

One day Frank and Jesse and Bob and Cole were
 riding down the road
to home with saddlebags full of gold. And they
 came on a farm where a
woman was out doing dishes in the yard. They were
 all hungry so they
stopped and said,
 Say, ma'am, would you cook us some dinner,
 we are real hungry
 (They didn't have any restaurants in those days,
 my mother explains).
 And the woman said,
 Hell no, can't you tell a person's doing a laundry
 when you see it?
 But, ma'am, we are real hungry, and we will

The James farm, circa 1877, where Jesse James was born roughly thirty years before.

pay you for it.
No, I ain't going to do it, she said
But look here, you could cook us a chicken, I see you got a lot of
chickens there and I'll even kill one for you.
And he whipt out his pistol and shot the head off a chicken.
Well now, since you done kilt that chicken you can just gut it, and
pluck it, she said. She was so mad she was hopping around the yard, lookt
like somebody killing snakes with a switch.
And all the boys razzed Jesse and laught at him and shoved him off

his horse and he had to sit down and gut and pluck
    that chicken. And she
went and fried it for them and charged them a high
    enough price for it,
I can tell you. And the boys never let him live it
    down, when they would
be riding hard away from the law and they saw
    some chickens somebody would
yell
    Oh, Jesse, I want my dinner, go shoot me that
    chicken. Oh, Jesse, we're
hungry, blow the head off that rooster, will you?
    There are good days and bad days in the life of
    a bank robber. My
mother swears this story is true. The farmer's wife
    was trying to teach
them that you have to eat what you kill.
    Think of yourself as a chicken.

PART II

WHO HAD KILLED MANY MEN

Not long after the end of the Civil War, a string of successful robberies catapulted the James-Younger Gang into the national spotlight. From an 1866 holdup of the Clay County Savings Bank of Liberty, Missouri (ten to fourteen members of the gang made off with as much as $62,000, killing a young bystander in the process) to a Missouri-Pacific job near Otterville, Missouri, the crimes were mostly well-planned, professional affairs and tended to target banks and railroads. It was said the gang invented a new profession when they derailed and robbed a moving train at Adair, Iowa. While membership in the gang was fluid and changeable, the participants were almost always former Missouri Confederate guerrillas. Due in part to lingering sympathy for the Confederacy as well as the sponsorship of Kansas City Times *journalist John Newman Edwards, Jesse James soon became a kind of "Robin Hood" figure. He worked hard to live up to his image.*

On the heels of their various "successes," however, came tragedy. The James family farm was assaulted in 1875 by parties likely associated with the Pinkerton Detective Agency. An incendiary device thrown into the cabin exploded, killing Jesse's half brother and wounding his mother, leading to the amputation of her lower right arm. The best of modern research on this incident, and the events leading up to it, are excerpted from Ted Yeatman's book, Frank and Jesse James: The Story behind the Legend.

On September 7, 1876, the James-Younger Gang was all but wiped out during an attempt to rob the First National Bank of Northfield, Minnesota. Jack Koblas's account of the actions of that day is excerpted here. Outside their typical area of operations, most members of the gang were either killed, wounded, or captured by the unsympathetic citizens of Northfield. Not long afterwards, gang member Charlie Pitts was killed and the Younger brothers were taken prisoner. Only Frank and Jesse James made a clean getaway back to Missouri.

Written histories of the James-Younger Gang began appearing as early as 1876. Two of the early accounts, by Frank Triplett and Jay Donald, are also excerpted here. These massive works constitute the foundation of much later scholarship and fiction.

It is three years before a reconstructed gang arises out of the ashes of Northfield. Most of the early members of the gang are dead, in prison, or have simply disappeared. New inexperienced men with little Civil War background are recurited and they are not as reliable or talented as the old members. These new men include Charles and Robert Ford.

— Harold Dellinger

FROM

UNDER THE BLACK FLAG

By Captain Kit Dalton, a Confederate Soldier

1914

We crossed the state of Texas and came to the Rio Grande a few miles from Monterey, where we found a little picturesque village to our liking on the banks of the boundary river. Here we deported ourselves as men of affairs and were most hospitably received when it became noised around that we were wealthy cattlemen of the United States, prospecting in their vicinity.

In a short while Jesse was able to make himself understood in their native tongue—at least he said he could and there were grounds for his claim, as he could go through their conversational calasthenics pretty well and was able to enterlard the vowel "O" in every word. But as for myself, had I remained there till this day, I don't believe I could have learned to call a dog in that outlandish tongue.

Being pretty well in funds and naturally of generous natures, we were liberal spenders and altogether handled ourselves as gentlemen of affairs. In this manner we engratiated ourselves in the favor of our associates, through whom we had access to the best homes and naturally got on the sunny side of the gentler sex, who seemed particularly fond of Jesse and by no means indifferent to my attempted blandishments.

For three weeks we moved in and out among the people in the most cordial social relations and were having the time of our lives when the gates of Paradise were suddenly slammed in our faces.

It came about in this way:

For our special benefit a Fandago had been arranged in some kind of an adobe shack, and we were in the midst of a mazy whirl when a greaser who had never looked with favor on our suave ways with the senoritas deliberately stepped on Jesse's foot in the exhilarating dance, and catching Jesse's eye, indicated by a nod of his head that he had done it as a challenge.

But the dance went on to the trumming of guitars, and when it was over Jesse came to me and told me of his experience with the greaser.

"What would you do about it?" he eagerly asked.

"Pass it up unnoticed," I replied, for we were certainly in no position to raise a rough house in such a land of treachery where every gallant carried his stiletto or bowie and was so proficient in the use thereof. It was a bitter pill for Jesse, but he took it down without water, and when the next dance was called, each of us had a languid-eyed, romantically-inclined beauty on our arm.

I was not more than ten feet from Jesse when I saw him jerk up his foot like he might have stepped on a hot iron, and his face was livid with pent up passion. The greaser, passing by, had deliberately stepped on it and was grinning with fiendish delight at the discomfort he had caused. In an instant Jesse subdued his passion and continued the dance, but only for a moment. The greaser repeated his devilish tactics with renewed force and venom. Instantly Jesse let go his modest hold of the girl, sprang at the greaser and jerking him by the collar, hurled him nearly across the room. In an instant he was up and his flashing blade was no more than three inches from Jesse's heart, when a well directed bullet stayed the further progress of the murderous blade and the greaser lunged backward, in his fall upsetting a dancing couple. This seemed to be the signal for a general attack, and before Wood and I could reach the side of our comrade knives were hacking at us from every direction, but when we three came together and formed a triangle with our backs to each other, it was a matter of physical impossibility to reach us with those carving sets. In this manner we shuffled along toward the door, sprang out, mounted our horses and five minutes later were on our very ungenerous Uncle-In-Law Sam's side of the stream.

How many we disabled in this little joust, I am unable to say, but this I do say, and that right sincerely—we shot no man nor hurt anyone but those who had their murderous blades at our hearts.

When we were out of harm's way and had time to deliberate over the unfortunate incident, we all, figuring in our own way, came to the conclusion that our conduct had aroused the jealousy of these passionate people and the dance was a decoy for our destruction. However, I must say in justification of the women, that they were in complete ignorance of the diabolical plot, for I sincerely believe that Jesse's bewitching little enamorata would have given him a tip and gotten us all out of the way for his sake.

Now what were we to do? Our dreams of peace "neath tropical skies" had vanished into thin air. The United States seemed to be a happy hunting ground for detectives and secret service men and we were the quarry.

"One country seems to be about as good for us as another," I remarked to Jesse as we rode along brooding over our unlooked for hard luck.

"You'd better say, one country is about as bad as another," suggested Jesse, and for the next few miles he seemed for one time in life down on his luck. I really believe thoughts of the little senorita had as much to do with his short lived spell of blues as anything else, for ever and anon he would draw a deep breath and say, "One of those devils will gallivant her home," or, "Wasn't she a peach?" Some such remark bubbling out every now and then made it very plain to me and Wood Hite that Jesse must have been pretty much enamored and that the greaser must have been the most aggrieved party.

FROM

JESSE JAMES WAS MY NEIGHBOR

By Homer Croy

1949

One of the marked characteristics of Jesse James was his humor. He liked to play pranks; rarely did he go through a robbery without doing or saying something that had an element of humor in it. A good illustration of this is something that happened in the foothills of the Ozarks. One day the James-Youngers were taking a back road when noon came upon them. It was their custom to go to a farmhouse and get the wife to prepare a meal for them. And they always paid well. (I have not been able to find a single instance where they rode away without paying, or offering to pay.)

They came to a humble cabin, and one of the group went to the door to ask the question. A woman answered the halloo, a bit startled to see two other mounted men. She didn't know whether she could cook the meal or not, she said, as there wasn't much to eat in the cabin. But finally she was prevailed upon. She watched the men dismount and seat themselves in the yard to wait till the meal was ready.

As the men waited they were more and more impressed by the poverty of the cabin and by the hard struggle the woman had to live. Then they noticed that the woman was weeping, and asked her if she was frightened. She said she wasn't, but that seeing men in her cabin made her think of her husband. It developed that her husband was dead and that she was having to face her problems alone.

The men were appreciative of this and, glancing at each other, decided to be liberal with her. Sensing this friendly sympathy, the woman choked up; she tried to hide her emotions but she was so wrought up that she was unsuccessful.

Jesse said, "Won't you tell us what's the matter?"

The woman hesitated, but at last the trouble came out. The cabin and her little farm were mortgaged to a heartless skinflint who had been pressing her for the money. He had warned her that if she did not have the mortgage money ready when he arrived, he would take her property.

"He's coming today," she said, again beginning to weep.

At last dinner was ready and the men sat down. Jesse, for the most part, ate in silence, now and then glancing at the poor widow in her humble surroundings. Finally he said, "How much do you owe this man?"

"Eight hundred dollars."

Jesse ate a few moments.

"When did you say he was coming?"

"This afternoon, about four."

Jesse took a few more bites.

"What does he look like?"

She told him.

"How will he be traveling?"

"In a democrat wagon, drivin' one horse."

At the end of the meal Jesse pushed back in his chair. "What road does he usually take?"

The woman told him.

"It so happens," said Jesse, "I have that much money with me and I'm going to loan it to you."

The woman looked at him in amazement. Was he joking?

He wasn't.

"You remind me of my mother," said Jesse, "and I want to do something for you."

The woman began to weep afresh. "I'll work my fingers to the bone, but I don't know when I can pay you back," she cried.

Jesse patted her shoulder. "Don't worry about that. I'll stop by some time, then if you have it, you can pay me back."

The woman sobbed anew at her guest's splendid generosity.

"Now you want to do this in a businesslike way," said Jesse. "He sounds like a hard man to deal with, so you ought to protect yourself. This gentleman here"—indicating Frank James—"will write out a receipt. Then you copy it in ink in your own handwriting. Before you pay over the money, you make the man sign the receipt. That's the proper way to conduct business. He'd make you do the same. And don't tell him anyone has been here. Now, will you do as I say?"

"Yes, sir," cried the weeping widow. "I think you're wonderful."

"I wouldn't say that," Jesse answered modestly. "I like to help deserving people when I can."

"He's a very kind-hearted man," explained Frank.

Finally the men mounted their horses. In the door the widow stood, her face alight, and waved goodbye to them.

That afternoon the skinflint called on the woman, signed the receipt, and left. After he had driven about three miles away from her cabin, on his way home, an unfortunate incident occurred. Suddenly three mounted men popped out of the timber; one seized the horse's bridle and all leveled cruel looking weapons at him. The man chanced to have $800 . . . but not for long. The horsemen appropriated it, then they whipped up his horse and sent it spinning down the road, leaving the mortgage-holder alone and on foot with the problem of catching his horse as best he could.

Then the three men rode away. No one knew where they went.

Library of Congress, LC-USZ62-38208

Frank James at the age of fifty-five.

FROM

WANTED!

By Arthur Winfield Knight

1988

Jesse James: Robin Hood

They say Frank and I
gave an old lady
the money
to pay her mortgage,
then took it back
from the banker
after he'd collected.
I like that story,
but it's not true.
I'm no Robin Hood,
but I'm not a bad man,
either. I do my best.
But they'll never forgive me
because I rode
with a guerrilla band

under Quantrill.
They murdered my little brother
and blew Ma's arm off
when they threw a bomb
into our house,
and I was ambushed
when I went in for amnesty.
Now they've offered
a five thousand dollar reward
for me, dead or alive.
That's a lot of money,
so I can't turn my back
on anyone,
and I never leave the house
without a gun.
I change my name
in every town we come to,
and we never stay long.
I keep telling Zee
we'll stop one of these days,
settling down,
but she just cries
when I say that.
I've never been a good liar.
We both know
there won't be
any rest for us
until they've hounded me
into my grave.
We'll never stop running.

FROM

OUTLAWS OF THE BORDER:

A Complete and Authentic History of the Lives of Frank and Jesse James, the Younger Brothers, and Their Robber Companions, Including Quantrell and His Noted Guerillas, the Greatest Bandits the World Has Ever Known

By Jay Donald

1882

Jesse courted his cousin, a young lady, quite handsome, well educated, of a gentle disposition. He thought her an angel. She is an orphan. Her uncle is a clergyman. They reside in Kansas City. Jesse and Zee were boy and girl together; attended the same Sunday school, day school, and singing school. They grew up together till the war, when, as in so many other cases, they were separated. He became a brave and daring soldier, and she worshiped his deeds; he became a reckless outlaw, and she would not believe it.

After the war they frequently met, and she had nothing but words of admiration and affection for Jesse, who, with all his sin, was always tenderly kind to her . . .

Frequently he visited Kansas City, and braved the police

and others who were lying in wait for him. At one time, while visiting the home of his betrothed, five officers headed by the sheriff, came there to arrest him. Always on the alert for danger, he discovered them in time, and concealed himself under a bush beside the doorstep, where he lay during the search, with a pistol in each hand, cocked and ready for service. The men searched the premises industriously; one came and stood on the step just over Jesse's head, but went away without seeing him. If he had seen Jesse then he probably would not have gone away, for Jesse had since said that he could have killed every man in the party, but abstained from doing so because he feared that Zee might get hurt in the melee.

In 1874 Jesse James and Miss Zee Mimms were married at the home of a mutual friend, Dr. Denham of Kearney, Clay county, Missouri, by the Rev. William James, of the M. E. Church South. This gentleman was Jesse's uncle and a relative of the bride. The party was select. Jesse had won a wife, and she had become an outlaw's bride.

Their wedding tour was a flight across the country to Texas. There were no orange blossoms nor white gloves, nor any other livery of bride and groom worn on that journey; no sweet girl friends accompanied the young wife on her lonely way; no merry jests nor joyous laughter cheered that nuptial tour. The happiness of the poor bride was held in constant check by fear and watchfulness; the ceaseless vigil of the refugee restrained the joy which should have filled the breast of her outlaw husband. Poor girl! She had left a quiet home and loving friends for a place beside her hunted lover; before her was anxiety and dread, a wandering life, perhaps privation—certainly dishonor. How much her love and fidelity were to cost her she had not guessed—or she was very brave—but if she ever regretted the choice she made; if there ever were moments in her life when she contrasted her lot with the freedom and happiness of her girlhood, and shuddered; if the man who so remorselessly murdered his enemies was ever cruel to her, she bore it heroically, and locked the secret in her breast forever.

In Mexico they remained nearly two years. A little child as innocent and sweet as ours, came to bless them. Jesse was often seen with it on his shoulders, capering across his ranche, while Zee stood watching the child and its father with all the tenderness and joy of a woman's love, and Jesse acting, if not repeating, the immortal words of Shakespeare:

> "The mistress whom I serve quickens what's dead,
> And makes my labors pleasures."

FROM

THE LIFE, TIMES AND TREACHEROUS DEATH OF JESSE JAMES

By Frank Triplett

1882

From Chapter XX

The Train Robbery at Gads' Hill

It was on the 31st day of January, 1874, that Gadshill [Wayne County, Missouri] had a visit. In the history of Gadshill any visit would have proved eventful; but this being no ordinary visit, the interest excited was stupendous. It happened in this wise. About 3 o'clock in the afternoon of the 31st, seven armed men rode into the hamlet, dismounted and tied their horses, leaving one man to guard them. Although no formal invitation had been extended to them, yet they made themselves quite at home, and showed that it was not a mere passing call they intended, but quite a lengthy, if not social visit.

Their first precaution was to scout through the village, not a very onerous task, and secure all of the inhabitants and visitors (amounting to seven or eight). This was a wise precaution on their part, for Piedmont, only seven miles distant, was a telegraph station, and any one who had the slightest idea of the situation could have slipped away to that point, and reached it in time, even if afoot, to warn the down passenger that there was danger ahead.

These prisoners were all put into the station-house and carefully guarded. A signal flag was now set on the track and the lower end of the switch was also opened, so that if, alarmed at any outward indication, the engineer should attempt to run by the station, a ditched train would be the result. But nothing of the kind occurred, and promptly on time the 5.30 passenger from St. Louis appeared, and noticing the signal to stop the engineer whistled "down brakes," and brought the train to a standstill at the platform.

The conductor, Mr. Alford, stepped off of the cars, was promptly halted, relieved of his valuables and run into the improvised lock-up. While one of the brigands was robbing the conductor, another one had covered the engineer and fireman with a huge revolver, and persuaded them to leave their cab and take a little walk into the woods.

Instantaneously with the work of these two was that of the rest. It consisted in two men placing themselves at the passenger car doors, while another searched the passengers and secured their money, watches, etc.

The safe in the express car next attracted their attention, and a sledge hammer being secured it was broken open and its contents taken. The mail bags were cut open and the valuable letters and packages taken from them.

While searching the passengers each one was asked his name and place of residence. The object of this was made known to one of the passengers, whose curiosity at this strange procedure so far overcame his fright as to cause him to ask an explanation. It seemed that in some way the robbers had got an idea that Allan Pinkerton, the Chicago detective, was on board. It was well for him that he was not, for had he been found it would have required no astrologer to forecast his fate. A bitter hatred existed between this detective and these men, who had so far invariably got the better of the notorious thief-taker.

When the robbers rode out of Gadshill, after releasing all of their prisoners and bidding the engineer and conductor to "pullout," it was black night. No pursuit was attempted from Gadshill, but the train thundered on rapidly to Piedmont, and telegrams were sent in all directions warning every one to be on the lookout for these outlaws. At Piedmont, also, pursuit was organized and the bandits followed to Current river. Even at this distance, only some sixty miles away, two of the outlaws had "vanished into thin air," leaving but five. It is needless to say that the pursuit failed. These were undoubtedly the same men who had robbed the Hot Springs stage shortly before.

Chapter XXI
Whicher's Death

The flight of the Gadshill outlaws was continued on through a sparsely settled country; that of South Missouri, from Current river to the Big Piney in Texas county. They were still five in number, and seemed to be making for some point in the Indian Nation. Taking Bentonville, Arkansas, in the line of their retreat, they seemed so little to fear pursuit that here another outrage was committed. Bentonville lies in the tier of counties which join Missouri, and is just below the spurs of the Ozark mountains. It is a small town, prettily situated, and surrounded by a fairly rich country.

On the afternoon of the 11th day of February the retreating robbers had reached this placc, and riding to the store of Craig and Son, they dismounted and entered. With drawn revolvers they enforced quiet on the proprietors and clerks, took all of the money, about two hundred dollars, and helped themselves liberally to such goods as they fancied. They next threatened every one with death if any alarm was made, went out, mounted, and were off. They did not seem to be in any great haste, and when a few pursuers took their trail shortly after, they accomplished nothing.

These three outrages against the majesty of the law and the safety of the people occurring in such rapid succession, and the desperate boldness of their perpetrators, thoroughly aroused the ire of the authorities of Arkansas and Missouri, as well as of the officials of the railway and express companies. Even the United States put its reserve men of the Secret Service at work, determined if possible to repress this rapine and violence.

The States sent posses to the field; the United States its most efficient men of the Secret Service; and the railways and express companies employed the detectives of Chicago and St. Louis. The combination was certainly a most formidable one, and every one now predicted the capture or annihilation of the outlaws.

The trail of the robbers was taken and followed toward the Nation. Here, just at the line, a new idea seemed to have struck them, for they turned towards the north, always by the most secluded routes, on up to and through St. Clair and Jackson counties. Here a division took place, some of the band dropping out here; others continuing on across the river. They had separated and disappeared; it almost seemed as if the earth had opened and swallowed them up.

Pinkerton, incited to furious action by his continual failures, which were greatly injuring his boasted infallibility, determined to secure these men at any cost, so he sent his picked men to Missouri; even sending his brother, William Pinkerton, to Kansas City to establish a headquarters there so that operations might be simplified and results rendered more certain. Captain [Louis J.] Lull, with several assistants, was detached to operate against the Youngers on the south side of the river, while Whicher was to communicate with Jack Ladd, who had been placed at Daniel Askew's, in the immediate Samuels' neighborhood, a year before. This Ladd must have been a man of iron purpose and consummate dissimulation, for he was never for one moment suspected by the Jameses. Working at Askew's as a common hired hand, he was conveniently situated to spy upon the Samuels' household, and could give sure and speedy information of the presence at home of these dreaded outlaws.

When these arrangements were all consummated, Pinkerton is said to have rubbed his hands and said with great glee: "I've got 'em now!" The detective, as the sequel shows, had reckoned without his host. Had the men against whom he plotted been the ordinary thieves of large cities, he would have undoubtedly trapped them; but here he was matched by men of equal or greater skill, more endurance and overpowering bravery. Their unscrupulous readiness to take life was no greater than his, probably not so great, as witness his agents' killing of Little Archie Samuel.

Captain Lull and two others hunting for the Youngers were overtaken by two of their intended victims. Covered with a shot gun, they were ordered to drop their pistols. This they did. One of the Youngers got down to pick up these arms, and John Younger dropped his gun for a moment to quiet his horse. He had made a fatal mistake, for Lull, who was a man of undoubted bravery, hurriedly drew a concealed derringer and fired, striking Younger in the neck, the ball completely severing the jugular vein. It was, of course, a death wound, but so great was the vitality of the man, and so determined his bravery, that in his death agony he drew a pistol and fired, the ball passing through the left arm and into the left side of Lull. Reeling from his saddle he fired twice more, and he and Lull fell at the same instant.

Jim Younger then opened fire on Daniels, who returned it, striking Younger and causing a trifling wound. The next shot of Younger struck Daniels in the neck, and he fell dead. The third detective had already fled.

But to return to [John W.] Whicher. After having all the information possible put into his possession, a line of action was determined on, and he departed to Liberty, in Clay county, in order to consult with the officials there.

He called at the bank, stating his object to the president, Mr. [D. J.] Adkins, and was by him advised to consult with Col. [O. P.] Moss, a former sheriff, who could give him full and reliable information. On going to that gentleman and laying his plans before him, Whicher was advised not to undertake the desperate mission.

"You do not know," said this kindly gentleman, "the nature of the risk you undertake; nor can you, who have heretofore dealt only with the ordinary criminal classes, begin to comprehend the cunning and ferocity of these men, who have been educated to combat and strategy as no other men ever have. You need not hope to surprise them; at best you can only hope to elude their suspicion, lucky if you succeed in this. From being continually hunted and trailed by their enemies, it has become almost intuition with them to distinguish an enemy, and, as for daring bravery, they by far surpass any idea you may have formed of them as desperate men."

With such earnest entreaty Col. Moss sought to dissuade Whicher, but in vain.

"I have undertaken this work with my eyes open," said he, "and while I thank you for your evident kindliness, yet I can't help but think you overrate the men and the danger of attempting their arrest."

The Scotch say: "A willful man must have his way"—and so, seeing that Whicher, incited by the hope of earning the large rewards offered, would go, the colonel refrained from further entreaty; and Whicher, after changing his clothes, shouldered an old carpet-sack, and taking the afternoon train, soon reached Kearney, a small town within three miles of Dr. Samuel's farm.

Getting off at this place, he enquired for farm work, and then struck out on the road toward Dr. Samuel's. It was growing late in the afternoon, and he found the road a lonely one. He must have been a man of but little nervousness, or the solitary road, winding along the creek and overhung in places with steep bluffs and high, sombre and overreaching woods, must have cast a gloom over his spirits. The allurements of the immense rewards offered, and a cool, undaunted nerve, however, stimulated him, and he walked lightly along, noting every object and every suspicious circumstance, until at last, in passing a dense thicket, a figure confronts him with a drawn revolver.

Ah! Whicher, Fate has overtaken you. Your days on earth are now numbered, but be cool, match the cunning of the guerrilla with the cunning of the detective; the nerve of the outlaw with that of the thief-taker. Do not falter in a single particular—if you do, 'tis death.

Standing grimly in his path, the man with the revolver asks him his business.

"I am seeking work," said Whicher. "I want to get a place on a farm; do you know of any?"

"Yes," said the outlaw. "I know a place for you; a place you will keep all of your life, G— d— you!"

"Why, what's the matter with me?" asked Whicher; "what have I done?"

"Enough," said the outlaw, "but come with me," pointing to the woods.

To this command Whicher demurred, saying: "Why should I leave my road at your command? I am a free man and under no obligations to follow you. It is now growing late and I must find some place to rest to-night. If you know of any work I can get, tell me; if not, let me go on my way."

At this point of the dialogue three other armed men appeared on the scene.

"What's the use of bothering the man," said one; "why not kill him here, so we can go on? You know we must be home to-night, and it's a long ways to go."

"No, damn him," said the first bandit, "I've got a few questions to ask him, and he's got to answer them."

Whicher, thinking he might still deceive them, as he had no papers, badge, etc., upon his person, consented to accompany them.

"All right," he said, with a forced smile, "rather than have words about it I'll go with you."

Turning from the road, they all walked back about a quarter of a mile to where a steep bluff overhung a bridle-path in the dark woods.

Here they halted, and the first outlaw, who was no other than Jesse James, began to question the detective.

"Who are you, and what are you doing in this part of the country?" he asked.

"I am a poor man looking for work," responded the detective.

"These are d—d fine hands for a laborer," said Jesse, as he took one of Whicher's hands and examined it.

"I have not always been so poor," said the detective, hoping to excite some sympathy.

"No! nor you ain't so terribly poor now," said Jesse, turning to the other outlaws.

One of these now stepped up to Whicher and searched him, finding, in an inside breast pocket, a heavy Smith and Wesson's revolver. This discovery seemed greatly to enrage the outlaws, and one of them was for killing him immediately.

"No," said Jesse, "I want to ask him some questions; are you from Chicago?" said he to Whicher.

"No, sir!" said the latter.

"Where, then?" asked James

"From Indiana, sir!" (Whicher's former home.)

"I suppose you'll admit that you are a G—d d—d detective of Pinkerton's," said James.

"No, sir! I am not," said Whicher; "and even if I was, I've never done you any harm."

"No; but you'd like most d—d well to," said Jesse.

"Now, I want to lay down the law to you," he continued, "so that all of your tribe may know how I deal with you fellows who hunt men for money. I know you are all a pack of thieves, from Pinkerton down. I've been in cities, and know that they select all of their detectives from amongst thieves, who are mean enough to turn traitors to their companions. Now, this of itself is enough to condemn you to death, and the fact that you risk your life for money ought to make you willing to submit to it."

Seeing murder in the outlaw's eyes, Whicher poured out a prayer for mercy that was eloquent in its despair. He pleaded not for his life as a coward might, but that he might be spared to his young and loving wife. He painted such a scene of devotion and the suffering his death would entail upon a loving woman, that Jesse lowered his revolver (thinking, no doubt, of one as dear to him as this, as so soon to become the wife of a man whose occupation was as dangerous as that of Whicher), and said: "I can't do it, boys; it's no use talking."

"But I can," said one of the gang, a low, swarthy, ill-favored fellow with a big moustache and high cheek bones, and he drew his revolver.

"Not on my side of the line, Dick!" said Jesse, "not on my side of the line" (river).

"All right, then," said a tall, smoothly shaven man, "we'll take him over the line and do it."

Whicher, seeing that his death had been determined upon, begged Jesse to save him, but the latter, turning away, said: "It isn't for me to say now, ask the rest."

Frank James was not present at this scene at all, although numbers assert that he was an actor in it. When Jesse turned away, the other three tied Whicher's hands securely, placed a gag in his mouth, and taking him a short distance to where their horses were concealed, he was placed on the saddle of one of the horses, his legs tied together under its belly, and the small robber, called Dick, mounted behind him. Regaining the road, they pressed on towards the Missouri river, crossed it, and taking Whicher out into the timber near Blue Mills, they there rode under a tree standing near the road. Here the small man produced a piece of rope, tied one end of it around Whicher's neck, and standing up behind him on the horse, secured the other end of it to a limb of the tree. Alighting, he next cut the rope off of the detective's legs and led the horse out from under him, and left him suspended in air. After watching him for some minutes to assure themselves that he was dead, they rode off, firing back at him several times. As they rode off the smallest of the three remarked: "No tender spot in me for a damned detective."

One of the balls fired back at the body must have struck the rope by which it was suspended, for when found, it was lying in the road, a small piece of rope around the neck, another on the limb above it.

As every one knows, the Jameses have everywhere been accused of this murder; but this is not so, for Frank James was not present, and, for the second time in his life (the other will be related in another portion of this book!) Jesse seems to have given way to the angel whisperings of his better nature, and was willing that his enemy might go in peace.

In speaking of it afterwards, Jesse said:

"If I had killed him before he spoke of his wife, I would never have regretted it, for he was hunting me, and he was a detective taking the chances on his life for the sake of making money, and he had no right to 'squeal' if he got taken in, instead of taking in his man—but," he added, meditatively, "I couldn't do it when he spoke of his wife and how she'd suffer—I couldn't do it!"

Had Whicher known that one of the very men, who accompanied him in his lonely midnight ride to a terrible death, was in Liberty the very day he landed there, he might to-day be alive and happy. But fate willed it otherwise.

At the depot when Whicher's train came in was a plain-looking countryman, who seemed to know no one and who kept his own counsel. Seeing a stranger get off of the train, whose metropolitan air clearly indicated that he was from some city, this plain-looking farmer thought it might be as well to watch his movements. This he did in a slouching, careless manner, not calculated to attract the attention of any one. Seeing the stranger enter the bank, he took a station outside and watched his next move, a hasty glance into the window having showed that the stranger was depositing money.

Leaving the bank, the stranger was next seen in conversation with Col. O. P. Morse [Moss], who was most certainly not a friend of the Jameses. After this conversation was concluded, the stranger disappeared for a short time, and was next seen disguised in a laborer's suit of clothes on his way to the depot, where he took the train to Kearney and to death.

The rest is easily told. The countryman hastened to the Jameses and warned them to be on the lookout, and was even present when Whicher was captured.

Had this detective succeeded in passing unobserved to Askew's, and then joined forces with Jack Ladd, a desperate combat might have been fought between them and the outlaw brothers; but the "sleepless eye" of the detective was never yet proved a match for the wary cunning and watchfulness of these bandits.

FROM

SPEECHES AND WRITINGS OF WM. H. WALLACE

By William H. Wallace

1914

I did not write the indictment against Frank James above referred to, and I am not absolutely positive now what particular person he was charged with killing. I believe this is the only instance in which memory has failed me since I began to relate the facts. In changing the records from one room to another at Independence it seems the indictment has been lost, and after a search the clerk and myself can not find it. But as I now recall it was for the killing of J. W. Whicher, a Pinkerton detective from Chicago. Whicher, it was said, went to a banker in Liberty, Mo., supposing all bankers to be against the Jameses, and asked the way to the James' or Samuels' farm; said he was going there to hire as a farmhand and arrange for their capture. The banker reported his coming. As soon as he arrived he was tied, gagged, put on a horse, his feet tied together under the horse and conducted across the Missouri River on a ferry boat, and when within about two miles of Independence shot and left lying in the road. The body was brought to Independence. I was then a newspaper reporter, and wrote up the matter. I remember the dead man had a tender complexion and hands like a city fellow's, but was dressed much like a farmer. I pulled up the blue flannel shirt above his wrist and saw "J. W. W." in indigo ink on his arm. Of course there was no suggestion then as to who killed him, and I thought nothing about its having been done by the James band. The above account of the killing was given me by Liddil as he learned it from the band, as the deed was done before he joined the band. He said Jesse James told him the facts. He said Frank never admitted to him or to any one else, so far as he knew, that he, Frank, had ever committed any offense, and he only knew as to the deeds committed by Frank when he, Liddil, was along with him. I now recall distinctly that as prosecuting attorney, I investigated as to the killing of the Pinkerton man and his having been brought across the river gagged, with his feet tied together under the horse as above related. I summoned the ferryman who remembered that two men crossed a man on his boat one night gagged and tied as above indicated, but he said he did not recognize the two men. In other words, I found upon thorough investigation that I had no sufficient proof, and Frank was taken to Gallatin for trial.

FROM

COLLECTED POEMS

By Max Douglas

1978

The Perils

He never travels twice
the same road.

He never tells
the direction frm wch he came

nor the direction
in wch he means to go.

There is a design in this—

FROM

FRANK AND JESSE JAMES: THE STORY BEHIND THE LEGEND

By Ted P. Yeatman

2000

Around 7:30 P.M. on Monday, January 25, 1875, a train approached the town of Kearney on the Hannibal and Saint Joseph Railroad line. It was unusual in that it consisted of only an engine, a tender, and a caboose. Its destination was strange as well, a wooded area two miles north of town, out in the middle of nowhere. When the train stopped, a party of men, variously estimated at between four and eight in number, left the caboose and headed south through the newly fallen snow, cutting across toward the James-Samuel farm after apparently joining other men who had brought horses.

What happened next is perhaps best described first in a January 27 letter sent by Allan Pinkerton to Patrick Henry Woodward, chief special agent for U.S. Post Office Department:

> After great precautions and being positively assured, that the James boys and other of their friends,

were at home in their mother's house, near Kearney, Clay Co., Mo. Then having failed so many times, but this time every thing appeared perfectious, for we were sure they were in the house, on Monday, Jan. 25th at 5 p.m.

I today send a newspaper to Mr. Jewell Postmaster General, Mr. Corchrane [Charles J. Corchrane, division superintendent of Special Agents, Mail Depredations], and yourself, containing exaggerated details of what has taken place, all of which comes through Kansas City, a bitterly conservative state.

On Monday night every thing was ready. We were well supplied with Greek Fire, balls of cotton well saturated with combustible material.

After getting things ready we advanced on the house, not a word was spoken, and about half past twelve mid-night we commenced firing the buildings. But judge of our dismay, when we found every window fastened on the inside with wooden boards. although so concealed by a curtain that they could not be seen from the outside. When we threw the fire balls in, they fell harmless. Such is the manner in which the house is kept, it is a perfect citadel, however my men were equal to the occasion and soon battered in the windows, then flung the fire balls into the house, wild crys of dismay were heard from the inside, and soon the residents ran from the inside, which was lit up as light as day.

Mrs. James, or as she is better known by her present name Mrs. Samuels, was bitter in her denunciations, and used any-thing but polite language. I had given positive orders that no harm was to be done to the women or Dr. Samuels, and no one else was there. We stopped half an hour and saw everything plainly, so the men we were in search of must have left the house after dark. I am informed by telegraph that there is great feeling in regard to this business. One thing I am certain of, that is the same house, about one year ago, poor [Joseph] Whicher, my detective, was bound and gagged, then taken to

Independence, or near that place, and foully murdered.

I do not know what I will do next, I shall have to take time to consider my men in Louisiana and Texas. I shall continue for a short time, but I must say that I am considerably disheartened.

It is rather hard on me spending money continually, and then not finding them. It's too much for me, and I may probably withdraw, but I have not yet decided.

I hasten to lay the matter before you, and you will please consider it as strictly confidential.

In haste Yours Truly,
Allan Pinkerton

The story was not quite as simple as Pinkerton explained it. Pinkerton's men had taken position around the outbuildings near the house, the barn to the northwest, and the icehouse or smokehouse to the west of the house. Using "hollow tubes shaped like a Roman candle, and filled with combustible material," the detectives first attempted to set fire to three or four places on the weatherboarded northwest side of the house, which served as the kitchen and servants quarters. The tubes probably contained Levi Short's 1863 patented solid Greek fire. However, there were thick logs underneath, which the fire only scorched before Dr. Samuel, awakened by the cries of the black cook and her children, managed to extinguish the blaze by tearing off the boards. Mrs. Samuel was aroused by then and made her way around the house, the west section being locked from the inside. Entering the door on the north side, she found "something like a bowl of fire in the middle of the floor," along with a burning quilt on the bed. She tossed the quilt outside and tried to remove the flaming fireball, some seven and one-half inches in diameter, but it was too heavy. Then her husband came in and tossed it in the fireplace with a shovel. Next there was an explosion, and a portion of the shell struck Mrs. Samuel in the right wrist, shattering the bone. Another fragment hit thirteen-year-old Archie Peyton Samuel in the midsection. Another piece reportedly struck Dr.

Samuel in the head, but only stunned him. Archie later died of his injuries, and Mrs. Samuel had the lower portion of her right arm amputated.

The coroner's inquest the next day found that Archie's wound, in his right side, was "inflicted by the bursting of a shell thrown in the house. . . by some unknown person or persons." Tracks in the snow led to the point where the train had stopped. Before leaving the farm, the detectives had also fired around five shots. There was at first speculation that there had been a gun battle between a bandit and the detectives, but most likely these were only parting shots to keep those in the house at a distance. Blood was found along the trail and was later determined to have been the result of a possible cut or nosebleed, not a gunshot wound.

Another train from the south, identical to the one that had stopped earlier, arrived in the same general location about 2 or 3 A.M. When the Pinkerton men returned to the train, the conductor asked, "What success?"

A weary detective replied, "Don't ask us; don't say anything about it."

The train, heading east, was spotted at several locations with around eight men on board as passengers. Around 2 P.M. on January 26, it was reported to be at Ottumwa, Illinois, where the express "special" pulling the caboose was last seen, carrying men ranging in age from thirty to forty-five. A large crowd was kept at a distance as four of the men from the caboose obtained provisions. It was noted that the train was kept "fired up" all the time and sped rapidly out of the station.

Some days later the *Saint Louis Republican* noted the legal ramifications of the situation. Capturing or killing one of the outlaws on the James property would have established that the Samuel family had harbored fugitives of the law, and the family would have been "without the pale of legal protection." But failing to establish that the outlaws had been harbored by the family meant "the detectives would become subject to prosecution for homicide." However, Pinkerton's earlier letter stating that it had been his intention to "burn the house down" indicated his apparent plan to mix business with revenge. But the former barrel maker had miscalculated, and now he and his men were viewed by many as murderers and arsonists. It all played quite well into the hands of John Newman Edwards of the *Saint Louis Dispatch*, who rose to the occasion with one of the classic "ninety-proof" editorials of his career:

> If, as the telegraph reports this morning, Chicago detectives or any other detectives surrounded and set fire to the house of Mrs. Samuels, the mother of Jesse and Frank James, threw a hand grenade through the window and into the midst of a family of helpless and innocent children, the citizens of Clay county owe it to their self-protection and manhood to rise up and hunt the midnight cowards and assassins to their death. Such a species of warfare is worse than any yet painted of savage nature of the dastardly dogs who were hunting human flesh for hire, and who, although the men they sought were only two, even if they were at home, dared not meet them six to one and kill them in an open fight or bring them in as prisoners for a mob to hang or a fanatical public opinion to condemn and execute without trial. Men of Missouri, you who fought under Anderson, Quantrill, Todd, Poole, and the balance of the borderers and guerrillas—you who live in Clay county, and Jackson, and wherever these detectives have dared to leave the railroad to go into the country, recall your woodcraft and give up these scoundrels to the Henry rifle and Colt's revolver. It is not for the robberies that Pinkerton hates the James brothers. It is because like you they were at Lawrence, Centralia, and Fort Lincoln [Baxter Springs], and upon the Canadian, and wherever the black flag floated and men neither knew or wanted quarter. The monstrous crime of attempting to destroy a whole family in the heart of Missouri because two members of it have been accused of acts believed by half the state to be false and slanderous, is something that calls for redress. To set on fire a house in which women and children are sleeping, to throw a bomb-shell into it in order that through ignorance it may be permitted to explode amid a group of innocent boys and girls, are

> things too horrible to be tolerated. Surely none of Mrs. Samuels' neighbors were there and in the midst of the assassins who had surrounded the house. If they were and the names of them are ever known, the devil will help them all and save them from the vengeance of the sons. Meanwhile we await further particulars before we can understand fully the diabolical nature of the plot or who were engaged in it.

Edwards brings up the interesting point of culpability.

On August 6, 1874, James R. "Jim" Reed, a former Clay County native who had served under Quantrill and later turned to postwar outlawry, confessed on his deathbed that he had led the gang that robbed the train at Gads Hill and that the James brothers and Arthur McCoy had nothing to do with it. Reed had been shot in Texas by Deputy Sheriff John Morris. While Reed's confession may be open to debate, it is almost never mentioned in regard to the Gads Hill affair.

The killing of Detective Joseph Whicher is another matter, however, and the evidence here pointed very strongly in the direction of at least one of the James boys and their confederates.

Jesse James had been reported in the vicinity, perhaps even at the Samuel house the night before the Pinkerton raid and was suspected to be lurking somewhere nearby. On August 29 a new figure, or rather a bit of an old one, entered the picture: the newly elected sheriff of Clay County, John S. Groom. This was the same John Groom who had attested in an affidavit that Jesse had purchased items from his store at Kearney on the evening before the Gallatin robbery in which John Sheets had been killed. In his affidavit Groom had called Jesse one of the most honest persons he had ever dealt with.

Groom was not someone to be trifled with, though. Born in Clay County in 1828, he had served in the Mexican War as a corporal in O. P. Moss's Company C, First Missouri Mounted Volunteers, taking part in Alexander Doniphan's epic campaign through New Mexico and into northern Mexico itself. During the Civil War he had sided with the

KEN WHITE, PHOTO

A fragment of the Pinkerton bomb that killed Jesse's half brother and caused the amputation of his mother's arm.

South, raising a State Guard company and rising to the rank of captain. Just prior to the battle of Lexington, the company had joined Sterling Price for that engagement and the battle of Pea Ridge. Groom returned to Missouri in the summer of 1862 and took part in small battles at Independence and Lone Jack. He was wounded in the ferocious fighting during the latter engagement and barely escaped with his life. Groom tried to raise troops after his recovery then wisely decided to sit out the rest of the war in Colorado and Nebraska, engaging in mercantile pursuits there. Perhaps two wars were enough for him; he left when the conflict was starting to get extremely nasty.

Groom was apparently serious about his job as sheriff, however, and on Friday afternoon, August 29, he staged his own raid on the Samuel place. A posse of forty-six men had been scouring the county ever since the raid by the Pinkertons. On Friday morning the posse split up, half going into the western portion of the county and the rest heading to the Samuel place. Groom further divided his segment into three parts on reaching the farm. His party covered the outbuildings, another under J. W. Courtney watched the house itself, and the third group under Capt. Oscar Thomason, whose horse had been shot by Jesse in 1869, entered the house to search it.

It had been rumored that an underground tunnel or hiding place existed at the house, but nothing of the sort was found. "The family seemed to be not in the least concerned during the search," by one account. However, a search of the barn turned up a very fine-blooded mare that was said to belong to Jesse. The animal was presumably confiscated. Several individuals also were taken into custody at the farm, including Ed Miller, the younger brother of Clell; George James, a cousin of the James brothers and son of the Reverend William James, who had married Jesse and Zee; Ed M. Samuel, nephew of Dr. Reuben Samuel, and William Fox, whose brother Dory was a notorious character who would later be arrested for the murder of Whicher. From her bed Mrs. Samuel told the boys, "They're just taking you down there to pump you: keep your mouths shut and don't tell anything you don't know."

The boys were eventually released, except for Fox, who had an arrest warrant pending for stealing the horse of a Dr. Scruggs, the Kearney physician who had treated Mrs. Samuel's arm and whose horse disappeared at that time. Ed Samuel had had enough of the hounding. "I am past 22 years old, I ain't married but if I get out of this I am going to be. . . . If I get out of this I am going to get the hell out of Missouri," he told a reporter shortly before his release. True to his word, he left the state, married, and settled near Clifty, Arkansas.

Responding to public outrage, the Missouri legislature, after lengthy and rather rancorous partisan debate, voted to authorize further investigation of the incident at the James-Samuel farm.

Stilson Hutchins, who introduced the resolution, was the key owner of the *Saint Louis Dispatch* and later in his career founded the *Washington Post.* One of the main points at issue was the sovereignty of the state, as it was reported that prisoners had possibly been spirited out of Missouri without proper extradition proceedings, something that could create a dangerous precedent if ignored. Governor Hardin assigned the investigation to Adj. Gen. George Caleb Bingham, better known for his paintings of Early American subjects such as county elections, boatmen on the Missouri, and Daniel Boone crossing through Cumberland Gap.

FROM

THE JESSE JAMES NORTHFIELD RAID: CONFESSIONS OF THE NINTH MAN

By John Koblas

1999

On Thursday, September 7, 1876, Edward Bill, his wife, and their two daughters, Maude and Luna, rode into Northfield by horse and buggy from their farm in nearby Waterford. Bill, who had spent three years with General William T. Sherman during the Civil War, visited the hardware store operated by A. R. Manning and was about to cross the street at about two o'clock so his daughters could visit their uncle Fred Shatto, who ran a grocery store.

Ten-year-old Maude noticed three horsemen riding across the bridge on the west side of town. As the riders passed the Bills, the youngster was impressed by the big hats and clean linen dusters the men wore over their riding clothes. Maude was also dazzled by the beautiful horses each of the men rode, noticing the bridles decorated with silver. Five more men rode into town from the south and met the others in front of the First National Bank.

"They came riding over the old Cannon River bridge, two by two," she recalled years later. "They were elegantly mounted with gorgeous saddles on sturdy horses. We saw a few of them come into the square first to look things over. We were suspicious."

The family had just reached Maude's uncle's store when shooting broke out less than a half-block away. Fred Shatto was physically handicapped and couldn't respond, but, when the shooting commenced, Edward Bill grabbed a pistol and ran into the street. Just as he emerged from the store, a shot hit the window directly above his head, shattering the glass. Amid the shouting and shooting, terrified Maude and Luna held onto their mother and begged their father to take them home.

"Father told me not to worry," recalled Maude Bill Ordway. "The men were trying to rob the bank and wouldn't hurt me. I wasn't very convinced."

Mr. and Mrs. Charles Gress and their twenty-year-old son, Harry, lived above the shoe store they operated directly across from the First National Bank. They witnessed riders galloping away from the bank up Division Street. When shots rang out, Charles grabbed his musket and rushed to the roof.

"[Harry] ran up the back way to see where [his mother] was, and she was at the front window to see what was all going on," recalled a family member. "He pulled her away and told her they would shoot her, as they were firing at all the men on the roofs. When he returned to check on her a second time, I guess he found her at the window. She couldn't resist all that excitement."

Margaret Ann Sumner was on her way home to Northfield from a visit to Canada that same day when newsboys ran through her train in St. Paul shouting "Big Robbery in Northfield" and "James and the Younger Brothers have shot and killed many Northfield residents." She became sick with worry, believing her husband, Ira, a photographer, might be among the dead residents. Great was her relief when she found him standing on the platform waiting for her.

"A close neighbor of mine in Northfield ran home on that

memorable day to grab his rifle, and Mr. Manning was credited with killing one of the two robbers shot that day," said Ira. Margaret's daughter said, "Father never got over regretting that he had gone hunting that day, for the prairie chickens were flying."

The town of Northfield lies about forty miles directly south of St. Paul on either side of the Cannon River. The river was spanned by a bridge at Fourth Street with the east end of the structure opening into a square that extended a block, about twice the width of an ordinary street. Running north and south, Division Street merged with Fourth, which formed part of the square. The bank building faced the south side of the square, located on the west side of Division. On the end facing the square in 1876 were two stores with the bank entrance situated at the rear of the building facing Division.

John W. North had chosen the site of Bridge Square to build a town in early 1855. By the end of the following year, he had constructed a dam, a sawmill, and a gristmill. The two mills provided lumber for construction and a place where farmers could have their grain processed into flour. The Ames Mill, built in 1869, pioneered new milling processes, which gave Northfield flour the highest rating at the 1876 Centennial Exposition in Philadelphia.

The first major downtown commercial building was constructed for $15,000 by Hiram Scriver, Northfield's leading merchant and first mayor. The Scriver Building, with its rough limestone exterior and Romanesque Revival arches, housed the First National Bank of Northfield. Across the alley from the bank stood two hardware stores owned respectively by J. S. Allen and A. R. Manning. On the eastern side of Division Street, opposite the bank in the Scriver Block, were a hotel and several stores. A young Northfield man, H. M. Wheeler, then a medical student at the University of Michigan, stood in front of one of these buildings at the time of the incident in question.

About two o'clock on September 7, Charlie Pitts, Bob Younger, and possibly Jesse James, rode over the bridge, crossed Bridge Square, and dismounted in front of the bank. Tying their reins to hitching posts, they strolled lazily to the corner and seated themselves upon some dry goods boxes in front of Lee & Hitchcock's store.

Cole Younger and Clell Miller rode up Division Street from the south. In seeing the newcomers arrive, the trio seated in front of the store walked back to the front of the bank and went in. According to Cole Younger, the three were to enter the bank as soon as he and Miller crossed the bridge, providing there was not a crowd of people near the bank. "When Miller and myself crossed over the bridge, I saw a crowd of citizens about the corners, our boys sitting there on some boxes. I remarked to Miller about the crowd and said, 'Surely the boys will not go into the bank with so many people about. I wonder why they did not ride straight through the town.' We were half way across the square when we saw the three men rise and walk up the sidewalk toward the bank. Miller said: 'They are going in,' and I replied, 'If they do, the alarm will be given as sure as there's a hell, so you had better take that pipe out of your mouth.'"

Miller was convinced there was going to be trouble and, having lit his pipe just prior to crossing the river, remarked he was going to smoke through the entire robbery. As the three men before him entered the bank, Cole looked over his shoulder and saw his brother Jim and two other robbers crossing the river. Cole and Clell were to remain in front of the bank and sound any would-be alarm should the local citizens get suspicious and arm themselves. His signal to the trio in the bank and those riding up would be a rebel yell. According to Cole, none of the gang were to shoot anyone. Shots would be fired only to scare people off the street.

Miller dismounted, walked to the bank entrance and closed the front door. Cole Younger stepped down from his horse in the middle of the street and pretended to tighten the girth of his saddle. Their awkward actions attracted the attention of some of the citizens. Many of these citizens had already heard that nine men had been seen coming out of the woods southwest of the city and the strange horsemen in and outside the bank were undoubtedly some of the same. Others laughed at their more suspicious brethren; their minds made up the men were merely cattle buyers conducting their business.

The fact that nine men, not eight, were seen coming out of the woods would certainly add credibility to Los Angeles Bill Stiles' account. With the eight others in town, he would have been left alone to guard the escape route at the bridge and would not have been seen during the robbery or subsequent flight.

Steven Budd, an eyewitness in Northfield that day later recalled, "On the day of the bank robbery I was on the sidewalk opposite the door of the bank in front of Gress' store when two men on horseback rode up to the side of the street I was on and hitched their horses a little to the north of me. I went out to them as I had beef to sell and thought they were cattle buyers and, looking at them, concluded that was not their business and went into Gress' store again. Soon after three others came riding up and throwing the lines carelessly over the posts in front of the bank went back around the corner of Scriver's store north of the bank and stood there awhile talking. They remained there probably ten minutes until three other horsemen were seen coming across the bridge when they turned and went quickly into the bank."

Another citizen, Norman Van Buskirk, was sitting in his shop on the west side of the river when he saw three horsemen riding across the bridge into town. Shortly after, Van Buskirk recalled five more horsemen cantering across the bridge. He wondered about the linen dusters they wore, which appeared to him as if the men wore some kind of uniform.

Mrs. E. P. Kingman also witnessed three men riding south through Division Street but, supposing they were cattle drovers, paid little attention to them. "I was on the side of the street opposite the bank near the end of the block," she later recalled. "They halted for a minute or two directly in front of Thorson's store, which was about four doors south of the bank, and then went towards the bank. My attention was then taken up with customers, and I lost sight of them probably for a minute or two."

But at least a few citizens were suspicious. Francis Howard was standing at the west end of the bridge when the first three horsemen came riding abreast over the river. "They attracted my attention by their dress and general appearance, and I turned and followed them across the bridge, probably a rod or a rod and a half behind," remembered Howard. "I followed them until about forty feet to the east of the bridge, where I met Elias Stacy, who stood on the sidewalk, looking at them. I was so near to them that when I spoke I had to speak very low so that they would not hear me. I said, 'Stacy, those gentlemen will bear watching,' and he replied that he thought so too."

Howard and Stacy followed the riders up the street but remained on the sidewalk. The riders proceeded to the corner where the bank was and tied their horses. The Northfield pair watched their movements from the opposite corner. The robbers then walked around to a store at the north side of the bank and sat down on a dry goods box. Two more riders soon rode up in front of the bank followed by three others who stopped in the center of the square on the north side. As soon as the trio stopped, the first three men got up from the dry goods box and entered the bank.

J. S. Allen and two other Northfield citizens were standing on the corner talking. Howard stepped up to them and said, "There is a St. Alban's raid." Allen quickly left the men, walked to the bank door and attempted to look in. Immediately, Clell Miller stepped out of the doorway and grasped Allen by the lapel of his coat. Miller quickly drew his revolver, and in swinging it over his head, began shooting a volley of shots into the air and shouting, "Get out of there, you sons of bitches."

Allen jerked free from Miller and ran towards a store around the corner, shouting, "Get your guns, boys. They are robbing the bank."

Citizen H. B. Gress saw Allen break free and knew immediately what was transpiring. "Up to that time I had no idea what was to occur," said Gress. "I hollered at once, 'they are robbing the bank.' And it was taken up from store to store until the whole business part of the town was aroused to the situation."

Meanwhile, H. M. Wheeler, who had been sitting in front of his father's drugstore on the east side of the street, had grown suspicious. He had witnessed General Adelbert Ames with his daughter leave the bank and walk toward the mill. After seeing three strangers go into the bank and two more in front of the building, he walked down to the bank. When

Minnesota Historical Society, Sumner's Gallery, Rice County. Northfield. Street Scenes.

The Northfield Bank (right) as it looked at the time of the robbery.

he saw Allen struggling with Miller, he began shouting, "Robbery! Robbery!"

Cole Younger and Clell Miller sprang into their saddles and shouted at Wheeler to get back. One of them shot at him as he ran back to the drugstore to get a gun. Unable to find the weapon, Wheeler left by the back door and ran up the alley to the Dampier Hotel on the corner. Rushing through the lobby, he grabbed the clerk's rifle and ammunition and took up a position in a third floor window.

Cole fired his gun in the air to let the riders coming up from the bridge know that the alarm had been given. In seeing Miller firing at

Wheeler, he shouted, "Don't shoot him; let him go." The other three horsemen rode up at a full gallop. Chadwell also saw Wheeler running away and was about to shoot, but Cole yelled for him to let the man go.

The two outlaws began riding up and down Division Street shooting in every direction while shouting for everyone to "get-in." The three riders who had come up from the bridge employed the same tactics shooting at any window where a head appeared. The robbers meant to frighten everyone away. As bullets sent glass shattering and terrifying shouts filled the air, the street took on almost an circus-like atmosphere.

There was to be a show in town that evening, so many of the people thought initially they were witnessing some sort of street exhibit. In the excitement, Nicholaus Gustavson, a Swedish immigrant who did not understand English, was mesmerized by the spectacle. He remained in the street watching the events after being warned several times by the outlaws to leave the scene. One of the robbers shot him, and he died several days later.

Gustavson had emigrated to the United States from Smaland, Sweden, and had been living on a farm with his brother, Peter, three miles west of Millersburg. He had come to Northfield on the day of the robbery to purchase supplies with some of his neighbors, Peter Youngquist, Mrs. Peter Gustafson, Mrs. Carl Swanson, and Mrs. Swen Olson. The Swedes always purchased their supplies in Northfield; it was closer than Faribault and had more to offer than Dundas. When the shooting began, Gustavson was in a store south of the bank, and he apparently dashed outside to see what was happening.

A Northfield citizen, John Olson, witnessed the death of Gustavson: "As I was working in a cellar under the building on the corner south of where the First National Bank then stood, I heard shooting. I immediately ran up to see what was going on and went to the crossing on Fifth Street, which intersects Division Street one block south of the square. Immediately, a man came up to me and, pointing a revolver and cursing me, ordered me to get away, calling me all kinds of names."

As the outlaw pointed the revolver at Olson, the Northfield man noticed a neighbor's little boy standing in the street weeping, and, as the father ran up and clutched his child, the outlaw turned away from Olson and began threatening the father of the boy. Just then, Olson saw a man fall on the other side of the street, and as the outlaw was distracted, he bolted down Fifth Street and returned to the cellar.

"As I turned to run in, a Swede named Gustafson [sic] came running up, and we met right half way between the corner and the stairway to the basement," said Olson. "The stairway is about twenty feet from the corner. Just as we met, a ball struck Gustafson and he fell backwards, striking me on the leg and staggering me. I kept on running to the stairway, however, but, on reaching the door, which was two steps below the street, I found it locked, so I squatted right down by the door. I began to think about the man who was shot and concluded I ought to help him down. I looked up and as soon as my head was above the sidewalk the robber caught sight of me and told me to 'sit right still where you are, or I'll kill you too.' I squatted down again, and the next thing I saw was Gustafson, who had been shot, run down towards the river."

Olson ran to assist the injured Swede who was washing himself in the stream, and helped him get to a doctor at the Norwegian Hotel. The physician found that Gustavson's skull had been fractured and the brain pierced by the bullet. According to Olson, Gustavson lived another four days while he and a friend cared for him.

Olson continued: "From the position in which Gustafson was when he was shot, it was physically impossible for him to have been killed by a ball from the guns of any of those defending the bank. The ball would have had to turn the corner about ten or twelve feet. The building was a stone one. I believe he was shot by the robber guarding the corner. He was there the entire time I was out of the cellar and was shooting all the time in every direction and was evidently set there to guard the corner."

Dr. D. J. Whiting also witnessed the shooting of Gustavson after seeing riders pass his office window in the north end of the bank building: "Soon I heard firing and saw doves flying. I thought the boys across the street were shooting and went to the doorway at the head of the stairs and saw several men on horseback riding up and down the street firing revolvers, swearing and yelling in the wildest manner. Some man, apparently a foreigner, was coming up the sidewalk. They wanted him to run but he only took a natural gait, which seemed to enrage one of the horsemen as he rode up near to him firing and ordering him off the street. About this time some of them saw me and sent a shot at me, ordering me back."

Dr. Whiting was unable to grasp the situation. Earlier that day, a lady in his office had told him an Indian show was planned for that evening that promised a great deal of excitement. But before he could gather his thoughts, attorney A. O. Whipple, whose office was located in the south end of the same building, rushed in with the news a gang of outlaws was robbing the bank.

Inside the bank, the first three robbers were negotiating with three bank employees: A. E. Bunker, teller; J. L. Heywood, bookkeeper; and F. J. Wilcox, assistant bookkeeper. Since the cashier, G. M. Phillips, was out of state, Heywood was serving as acting cashier. At the time, the bank was located in temporary quarters. A "store-type" counter stretched across two sides of the interior between the lobby and the room's interior. A tall railing with glass panels ran the entire counter length, but there was an open space, totally unprotected, where a man had ample room to pass through.

F. J. Wilcox recalled that afternoon when he was suddenly startled by a noise at the door, only to look up and find three men with pistols in their hands. One of the robbers commanded, "Throw up your hands. We are going to rob the bank." The outlaws jumped over the counter and demanded the three bank employees get down on their knees with their hands in the air. The bankers were then told there were forty robbers outside, and it was a bad idea to think of resisting.

Wilcox believed the outlaws did not see Heywood when they came in, as he was sitting off to the side at a desk with a high front that partially concealed him. When they demanded the cashier open the vault, Heywood jumped up and was promptly ordered to his knees with his hands up. According to Wilcox, the three outlaws were Bob Younger, Charlie Pitts, and probably Frank James. Wilcox was sure the men had been drinking because the smell of liquor was very strong.

While demanding the opening of the safe, the robbers went through the pockets of the bank employees, looking for weapons. When Bob Younger's hand struck a large jack knife in Wilcox's hip pocket, he remarked, "What's that?" Assured it was only a jackknife, Bob left him alone. The outlaws searched the office for a cash drawer but found only an open till on the counter, from which they appropriated a handful of small currency. The money was put in a grain sack, which was left on the floor.

Their attention was then drawn to the vault. One of the robbers stepped into the open vault, when Heywood, protective of the contents, jumped to the vault door and partially closed it. He was quickly seized and dragged away from the door. Bob Younger noticed Bunker had edged to the counter, and the outlaw jumped in front of him after noticing a small revolver on the shelf. He commanded Bunker to keep silent, and placed the revolver in his pocket. Bob bellowed, "You couldn't do anything with that little derringer anyway."

Grabbing Heywood, the outlaws insisted he was the cashier. Said Wilcox: "As they stood over him, one pulled out a knife, drew Heywood's head back, and said, 'Let's cut his throat.' I think the knife was drawn across his throat leaving a slight scratch. Then to further intimidate him a shot was fired over his head. About this time the leader ordered one of the others to go into the vault and try the safe. I believe it was Pitts who replied, 'All right, but don't let him [Heywood] lock me in there.' "

The recollections of A. E. Bunker differ slightly from those of Wilcox. According to Bunker, Frank James and Charlie Pitts both grabbed Heywood when he attempted to close the door of the vault and pointed their revolvers in his face. He was told to "Open that safe, now, or you haven't a minute to live."

Recalled Bunker: "Heywood replied, 'There is a time lock on, and the safe can't be opened now.' 'That's a lie,' retorted James and Pitts, and repeatedly demanded that he open the safe, coupling each demand with a threat, and commenced hustling Heywood about the room. Seeming to realize they were desperate men, Heywood called 'Murder! Murder!

Murder!' whereupon James struck him a terrible blow on the head with his revolver, felling him to the floor. Some think this would have killed Heywood had no other injury been inflicted. He fell perfectly limp, and could not have been fully conscious after receiving the shock, as no word escaped his lips. Pitts then drew a knife from his pocket, and, opening it, said: 'Let's cut his damned throat,' and drew the edge of the knife across poor Heywood's neck, inflicting a slight wound while he was lying helpless on the floor."

The outlaw pair then dragged Heywood inside the vault and again ordered him to open it. At the same time, revolvers were leveled at Wilcox and Bunker, and they too were ordered to unlock the safe. The robbers did not know that the safe was not locked at the time. With the door closed, the bolts thrown in place, the outlaws could not tell the dial was still tuned to the correct combination.

Growing angry, Pitts placed his revolver to Heywood's head and fired. The bullet struck a tin box of jewelry and valuable papers in the vault. While Pitts and James were intimidating Heywood, Bob Younger again turned his attention to the other two bankers. When Bunker had first thrown up his hands, he was still holding the pen he had been using when the robbers entered the bank. When he went to set it down, Bob Younger leaped at him and stuck his revolver into his face, telling him to keep his hands up or he'd kill him.

Younger then ordered the two bank employees to get on their knees behind the counter. Bob shifted his revolver from Bunker to Wilcox, then fumbled through papers on the counter top or in drawers. While on his knees, Bunker remembered the Smith & Wesson .32-calibre pistol on the shelf.

"I turned to see if I was near enough to reach the weapon, while Bob's back was turned to me, but Pitts happened to be looking my way at the time, and rushing across the intervening space, secured the revolver himself and coolly stuffed it into his pocket," recalled Bunker.

Bunker stumbled to his feet, thinking he must try and make some kind of defensive action or at least break away, get outside and sound the alarm. Bob Younger turned to him again and barked, "Where's the money outside the safe? Where's the cashier's till?" Bunker pointed to a box with partitions in it sitting on top of the counter, which contained less than $100 in nickels, pennies, and a little silver. He replied, "There's the money outside."

Below the box, underneath the counter, was a drawer containing about $3,000 in currency. Bunker did not mention that money nor did Bob Younger find it. Again, the outlaw ordered Bunker to get back down on his knees and keep his hands up. Reaching into his linen duster, Bob pulled out a grain sack and began transferring the money from the cash box to the bag. After dropping in a couple of handfuls, it suddenly occurred to him, according to Bunker that, "the claim he was working panned out but little."

Seeing Bunker still on his feet, Bob yelled, "There's more money than that out here. Where's that cashier's till? What in hell are you standing up for? I told you to keep down." He then grabbed hold of the banker and pushed him to the floor. Bunker did not resist. In doing so, Bob felt a large pocket book in Bunker's pocket. "What have you got here?" the outlaw shouted. After looking it over, he placed it back in the pocket, pressed his revolver to Bunker's temple and pushed him to the floor, again bellowing, "Show me where the money is, you sonofabitch, or I'll kill you."

Bunker was sure his time had come. Thoughts of his wife, his mother, and God flashed through his head as Bob continued to grip his shoulder. Seeing the banker was too frightened to answer, the outlaw released him and began another fruitless search for money outside the safe. Bunker stood up once more and noticed blood trickling down Heywood's face and neck from the wounds inflicted by Pitts. Since Heywood was prostrate, Bunker supposed the bullet had entered his head and killed him.

As Bob re-examined the contents of the drawer, Bunker started an escape move, despite the outlaw's gun pointed directly at him. The banker reasoned if he could get to Manning's hardware store, located west of the bank, across the alley, fronting Mill Square, the rear door of which was at right angles to the bank's rear door, he could sound the alarm. Of course, what was happening in the street might present another problem.

Wilcox was on his knees between Bunker and the door. Bunker motioned to him with his hand to move a little forward so he might be able to pass by. Suddenly Bunker dashed by him and, as he approached the doorway, Pitts, with a whoop, fired at him from the side of the vault. The bullet whizzed past Bunker's ear and through the blinds on the door. Bunker dashed out the rear door through what he later called, "the best opening for a young man I have ever seen." The weight of his body sprang the blinds as he crashed against them. Turning to the left outside, he descended some steps to the alley. But Pitts was in hot pursuit. Bunker pivoted again at the bottom of the stairs when a second shot from Pitts ripped through his shoulder as he ran opposite the rear entrance of Manning's store.

The shot had been fired from twenty feet away. It hit the fleeing banker's shoulder, barely missing the joint. The bullet passed through the shoulder blade and exited just below the collar bone, within half an inch of the subclavian artery. Dazed, Bunker remained on his feet. Unsure as to his condition, he did not jump into Manning's, but continued west instead through an open lot to Water Street and another block south to the home of a Dr. Coon.

"By the time Bunker started, I had heard shots outside, and from my position could see men riding up and down the streets shooting," recalled F. J. Wilcox, who had been still on his knees during Bunker's break to freedom. "Very soon after Mr. Heywood was struck down and then dragged toward the vault, the call came, 'Come out of the bank' followed by 'For God's sake come out; they are shooting us all to pieces.'" Pitts, re-entered the bank, then dashed back outside, followed by Bob Younger.

Out in the street, Cole Younger saw his brother Bob rush out of the bank. Assuming his other confederates were out of the bank, he jumped on his horse and started north to the corner of Bridge Square. At the square, he encountered a man upstairs across the street with a gun. To scare off this adversary, Cole fired a warning shot through a pane of glass above the man's head, and the man retreated out of sight. Cole later said he thought this man was Dr. Wheeler.

Cole then fired into the corner of the building to frighten away some people who had gathered by the outlaws' horses. They quickly ran around the corner out of sight. Cole saw Bob run down the sidewalk to get to his horse, and seeing that his brother was the only one to come out of the bank, he rode back to the bank and yelled again. His "For God's sake, come out," was the call Wilcox had heard from within the bank.

The last robber left the bank. Turning to go, he fired a shot at Heywood. The cashier staggered behind his desk and sank into a chair. Heywood's desk sat at right angles to the counter, and he sat sideways to the opening in the front with his back to the wall. As the robber leaped over the railing, he turned, placed his revolver against Heywood's head and fired. Heywood staggered forward, the bullet lodged in his head, and fell behind the counter leaving a pool of blood on the matting.

The blotter on Heywood's desk was smeared with blood and particles of brain, as was his desk. When the town's citizens entered the bank, they found the murdered man prone upon his face, blood and brains oozing from a hole in his right temple.

Joseph Lee Heywood left a wife and child to mourn his loss. Working in the place of Mr. Phillips, it had been his intent to leave with his wife for the centennial. He was formerly of Minneapolis where he was in the employ of Captain John Martin. When the bank of Northfield had opened four years earlier, he had accepted a position there, serving also as city treasurer of Northfield and treasurer of Carleton College. Heywood had accomplished these positions after being diagnosed as a hopeless consumptive ten years carlier.

But who had killed Heywood? Frank James, if he was indeed in the bank, had had his gun in his hand, and the cashier had deceived him. But Frank was known as being bitterly opposed to killing anyone during a robbery and later fought with his brother because Jesse was so ruthless. It could have been Bob Younger because he was drunk. When drinking, he was known to be too quick on the trigger. Cole would not let Bob stand guard outside the bank that day because of his inebriated state, and had ordered his younger brother to do no shooting inside the bank.

A Faribault attorney, who later visited the Youngers in Stillwater Prison, pointed a finger at dead outlaw Charlie Pitts as the murderer of Heywood: "I also heard them [the Youngers] say that Pitts was the man who shot Mr. Heywood as he lay on the floor. Pitts went into the bank with Cole, but he had been drinking quite heavily just before the raid." (This account of Cole Younger being in the bank contradicts several others.)

As Heywood lay dying inside, the streets of Northfield had turned into a battleground. Norman Van Buskirk was among those who answered the call of, "Get your guns, they're robbing the bank." Van Buskirk, who was then crossing the bridge, recalled: "One of the robbers came riding down the square, shouting, 'Get back you sons of bitches,' and shooting so close that I could hear the bullets whistling. I got back, making far better time than I did going over. When I got out of range I turned and saw that they were preparing to go away. . ."

Gilbert Onstad heard shots being fired and looked out his window. "I saw my little boy with another child walking along the sidewalk on the other side of the street," he recalled. "I ran out and when I was about in the middle of the street, a fellow on horseback rode up to me, and, calling me names and firing a revolver over my head, ordered me to step back. I ran by him and over to my boy and ran into the corner store in Scofield's building."

By then, the whole town was aroused. Guns were already loaded and ready because it was hunting season in that part of Minnesota. Guns popped out from upstairs windows and from around the corners of buildings up and down the street, as the robbers shot back, trying to keep the town at bay.

Said one historian, "The street at Northfield must have been pure confusion, terror, dust, smoke, yelling, shooting, horses running and jumping and neighing, people getting shot at, shooting at, dodging horses, perhaps dodging falling outlaws. . . "

The surprised outlaws found hell to pay for the scant sum for which they had committed murder. The bank later stated that $280 was missing. The bag of nickels Bob Younger had compiled had been left behind when things got hot outside. A linen duster was found in addition to the grain sack marked with the initials H.C.A. (A newspaper published a week later in referring to the duster and grain sack said, "Probably the bank would send these by express, if they could get their address.")

Dr. Wheeler, who had been one of the first to sound the alarm, had positioned himself in a second-story window when the fight began. Mr. Allen, meanwhile, had run to A. R. Manning at the hardware store and told him of the robbery in progress. Manning quickly grabbed a Remington rifle and some cartridges. Re-entering his own store, Allen shouted the news to his clerks. One citizen, Elias Stacy, who had been armed with a fowling piece from Allen, picked up a loaded shotgun and rushed to the corner where Clell Miller was remounting his horse.

Miller, directly in front of the bank, turned to face him, and Stacy surprised him with a full load of bird shot in the face. Miller was knocked from his horse but was not injured seriously, and Stacy ran for cover. Miller quickly jumped back on his horse, but Dr. Wheeler shot him from the second-story window. The bullet severed the subclavian artery and killed him.

Five doors from the bank, J. A. Hunt watched from a jewelry store. "I went to the door, and a man, Jim Younger, as I afterwards learned, rode up to within ten feet of me, firing with pistols in both hands, shouting and cursing, and ordered me back into the store. There were then three or four others riding up and down the street and one man still further south. As I went into the store, I saw one of the robbers shot and fall off his horse close to the sidewalk on the opposite side of the street. One of his companions, who was at the corner and whom I have since learned was Cole Younger, dismounted almost as soon as he fell and took the pistols from the body."

Only seconds before, Dr. Wheeler had taken a shot at Jim Younger who had raced by, but his aim was high, and the bullet missed the outlaw. Jim looked around to see who nearly hit him, but by then Dr. Wheeler had espied another target, Clell Miller. This time, he did not miss. Wheeler's third cartridge had fallen to the floor; useless because the paper used in part of its manufacture was torn. But Dampier, the hotel owner, came to his rescue with fresh ammunition. This time Dr. Wheeler hit Bob Younger in the right elbow as he rushed from the bank. But Bob was a seasoned outlaw and utilized the "border shift" in tossing his revolver into his left hand, ready for use.

Cole Younger later said he was with Miller and his own brother Bob when all hell broke loose. "Just then Miller called to me, saying he was shot, and, looking at him, I saw the blood running down his face," recalled Cole. "The firing by this time had become general, and as the two men in the bank had not yet come out, I was forced for the third time to ride to the bank and call to them to come out. And this time they did so. In the meantime, Miller had been shot again and had fallen from his horse. I jumped from my horse, ran to Miller to see how badly he was hurt, and, while turning him over, was shot in the left hip."

Cole said he took Miller's pistols, remounted his horse and, along with brother Jim, rode to Bob, who was standing near the stairway. At that moment, Bob was shot. Cole, seeing his brother switch his gun from right to left, knew Bob's limp arm was broken. "Bob ran up the street, and Jim helped him to mount," Cole continued. "I then called to Pitts to help me get Miller up on my horse in front of me. On lifting him up we saw that he was dead, so (I) told Pitts to lay him down again and to run up the street out of range, and I would take him up behind me."

Captain French, the town's postmaster, looked out on the once sleepy street that had come to life with a flurry of bullets breaking windows and ricocheting from stone buildings in long mean whines. French quickly locked his doors, closing the post office, and frantically searched for a gun. Unable to find a weapon, he stepped into the alley, picked up an armful of sizeable rocks, and began heaving them at the robbers. Soon Elias Hobbs and Justice Streeter joined him.

Also heeding Allen's call, A. R. Manning, who had been waiting on a customer, looked out his door as shots rang out. He saw a pair of horsemen galloping by firing their pistols. The hardware merchant quickly grabbed a rifle out of the window of his store, pulled the cover off, took a handful of cartridges and headed for the bank. As he ran, he loaded the gun.

"Very soon A. R. Manning came around the corner," recalled H. B. Gress. "Others were with him but he seemed the leader and displayed more real nerve than all the robbers put together. He stood on the corner after the citizens had driven them south on Division Street and faced them all, not knowing but they might attack him from the rear. The robbers at that time were hollering to each other, 'Kill the white-livered sonofabitch on the corner,' referring to Manning."

Manning later recalled: "As I turned the corner going to the bank, I saw two men on the opposite side of their horse, which was tied to a post. I knew they were robbers the minute my eyes struck them. I drew my gun on them, and as I did so they doubled right down behind the horse. Without taking my gun from my face I lowered the muzzle and shot the horse."

The shooting of the horse was witnessed by W. H. Riddell. "Two of the robbers laid down behind the dead horse and commenced shooting north down the street while one of them was under the bank stairs," recollected Riddell. "One of those behind the dead horse jumped up and ran to the bank door and shouted, 'For God's sake, boys, hurry up: It is getting too hot for us.' "

Manning quickly jumped around the corner to reload. In doing so, he found he could not pull the shell from his gun. He ran swiftly back to his store and chucked a ramrod through the rifle, releasing the shell. R. C. Phillips, another local citizen, had an explanation for the shell problem: "On the day of the Northfield raid, I was in the shop working for A. R. Manning. My shop opened directly on an eight-foot alley from the back door of the bank. The first thing I heard was some loud talking in the bank, and then I heard a shot. When I heard the shot, I started for the front of the store where Manning was working on his books. I asked Manning what that shot was and he said, 'I think it's that show that's going to be here tonight. I started to go up the corner where the steps were, when I met John Tosney and John Archer who shouted, 'They're robbing the bank.' At that time five men whom I saw on the bridge started to drive rapidly across the square, firing right and left and shouting, 'Get in, you sons of bitches.' I ran back into the store, took the guns and revolvers we had and threw them out on the showcase, handing at the same time a single shot Winchester to Manning. In doing so, however, I made a mistake and gave him the wrong size shells, so that after he went out and attempted to load his rifle he found he had to come back to get new shells."

But Manning returned to his position at the corner, again reloading as he ran. Seeing two or three robbers in front of the bank facing him, he fired a shot. The bullet hit a post that supported some stairs, but, in passing through it, it hit Cole Younger in the hip.

Manning was far from finished. Peeking around the corner, he found Bill Chadwell perched on his horse doing sentry duty some seventy to eighty feet up the street. More cautious now, he jumped back, reloaded and peeked around the corner. Taking deliberate aim, Manning fired. The bullet ripped through Chadwell's heart. The outlaw fell dead from his saddle, and the horse ran around the corner to a nearby livery stable.

James Law witnessed the shooting of Chadwell. After hearing shooting that sounded like "firecrackers on the fourth of July," he rushed up to the corner. "Then I saw Manning in front of Scriver's store in the rear of which the bank was, with his rifle pointed around the corner," he later remembered. "Immediately one of the robbers came riding down the street past the corner, and, seeing Manning with the rifle pointed, turned and shot at Manning while making the turn. Manning did not move but leveled his rifle, fired at the robber when he was near the corner. The horse carried him up the street for about 140 rods where he fell to the ground in front of Lockwood's store. That was all I saw; I came back to the west side of the river and gave the alarm, and when I got back they had gone. All the while I was on the street, the robbers were shooting and shooting right and left."

H. B. Gress saw the bandit fall: "A bullet from Manning's rifle struck him," Gress recalled. "He dropped to the side of his horse and turned and started back from whence he came, but soon fell off in the street and died there. The shooting produced such a concussion that frame buildings shook like trees would on a windy day. Anyone not being present could not imagine what an excitement the raid created and how people were terrorized."

Still another, A. H. Bjoraker, witnessed the demise of the Chadwell. Bjoraker watched as confused riders rode in a circle shooting and shouting. Taking a closer look, one of the robbers screamed, "Get in there, you sonofabitch, or I'll kill you." Jumping behind a pillar, the frightened Bjoraker continued to watch one of the men on horseback. "When he was right southeast of my store about in the middle of the intersection of Division and Fifth streets, I saw him drop his lines and the horse made a big jump and went north until he came to about the fourth store from the corner, where the man fell to the ground. I ran right over to him."

Manning then saw a man in the street halfway up the block who was staring at the opposite side of the street. Manning fired, the robber winced, and dashed around the corner. Then he saw a man on the sidewalk running toward him with a revolver in the air about to fire at him. Manning aimed his gun at him but the outlaw darted behind some boxes under the stairs.

Two or three times the men dodged each other. At this point, Dr. Wheeler fired from the upstairs window hitting the robber in the elbow. The robber, of course, turned out to be Bob Younger. Manning, however, did not know Younger had been shot by Wheeler, so he rushed back through his store and out the other side in an effort to come up behind the robber. By then the people of Northfield were coming out of buildings and Manning could not get off a shot at the fleeing Bob Younger who had sprang from his hiding place and mounted behind his brother Cole. The band, with two of its members dead in the streets of Northfield, turned and galloped out of town on the Dundas Road. They left $15,000 behind, still secure inside the bank.

Among the first citizens to reach the bank was M. W. Skinner who later recalled: "Looking over the counter, I saw Mr. Heywood lying there dead, his head resting about where the paying teller usually stood. I helped carry him home to his wife. I then went to the telegraph office to telegraph to Dundas, in which direction the robbers had gone, what had been done here and ask them to intercept them, but the operator at Dundas was not in and the message could not then be sent. When I went home at night my wife said to me that before she knew what to make of the noise; it sounded more like the popping of corn than anything else."

Ironically, among those with Manning during the gun battle was General Adelbert Ames, co-owner of the Ames mills, a stockholder of the bank, and a man despised by the James-Younger bunch. He just happened to be in town at the time and stood at Manning's back sharing the danger and advising his friend. Fifty-three years later he admitted his part in the Northfield affair: "Yes, it is true. I was with Manning while he, with his gun, was shooting at the murdering robbers who became, apparently, heroes. I was going over the bridge to the mill and met the James crowd going in the opposite direction. Shortly after reaching the mill, I heard someone shout, 'They are robbing the bank.' Returning, I saw Manning with his gun and joined him."

Ames downplayed his own role in the affair and gave Manning full credit: "Manning had a trembling hand but took deliberate aim and shot the moving horseman, nearly a block away, thru (sic) the heart and dropped him dead to the street."

In front of the bank lay the dead horse, the first to die. Near the horse was the body of Clell Miller, and only a half-block away on the opposite side of the street, reposed the body of Chadwell. Only the death of the horse moved the citizens who viewed the aftermath of the battle. On each side of them, shattered windows served as a grisly reminder of what had only moments before transpired; hitching posts, doors, window frames and store-fronts were riddled with bullets.

A woman who witnessed the scene later recalled: "I saw the bodies of three men lying in the dust of the street. Near them lay the body of a horse, one of those ridden by one of the robbers."

The scene inside the bank was no better with the bloodied body of

Heywood on the floor. His wife learned of the death quite by accident. She overheard a neighbor shout the news to another across the street. Although pained, the courageous lady in hearing the grisly details of her husband's death, said, "I would not have had him do otherwise."

A friend referred to Heywood as a shy, well-liked young man and was deeply moved by his passing. She later recalled: "I don't think there was such a thing as an ambulance in town at that time so they came for Mr. Heywood's body with a regular buggy. It was drawn up at the rear entrance of the bank. I saw the men carry out the body of poor Mr. Heywood and lay it in the buggy. Then they covered it over with a sheet."

The bodies of the two dead robbers were taken to be photographed in the studio of Ira E. Sumner, long time Northfield photographer. Both the dead robbers showed splendid physical development, and initially, it was thought they might even be brothers. One was six feet, three inches tall and appeared to be about twenty-five years of age. The other was five feet, eight inches, somewhat older than the other and more stoutly built. Both men had blue eyes and darkish, red, curly hair. A map with a route marked through LeSueur County was found on the body of the younger man. About $5.50 was found in their pockets as well as two gold watches.

Cole Younger later blamed the deaths on a quart of whiskey, which he concluded one of his men had concealed on the way to Northfield. Three of the men drank the whiskey in the woods during their separation the morning of the robbery. He said if he had known the men had been drunk, he would not have entered Northfield, since he was not a drinker and had no confidence in a man who was.

During the ride out of town, the last man to leave the bank conveyed to Cole what had happened to Heywood. As the outlaw jumped the counter in leaving the bank, he saw Miller lying in the street. At that moment, one of the clerks jumped up and ran towards a desk. The outlaw thought the clerk was going for a pistol, and he ordered him to stop and sit down. When the banker persisted and jumped from the counter, the killer leveled his pistol and fired.

"Cole Younger told me that the most unfortunate thing that could happen [was] that some people were getting rather suspicious of their being in the town, and that night six of the group managed to purchase a two-gallon stone jug of whiskey and stay drunk and noisy, which only increased the suspicions of their being in that town," recalled Cole's friend, Todd George. "Cole, at that time, was known to avoid drinking. Cole further said that the group with him was in no condition to successfully rob the bank. In an attempt to rob—when the discharge of arms was heard from the outside Cole made every effort to hurry them out of the bank and get out of the town, but they were rather slow in moving and just as they were leaving one of the group turned and shot the cashier . . . I have been asked so often if Cole Younger ever tole [sic] me who in the group committed the murder. On a number of occasions when I asked Cole if he could ever tell me who did this, his answer was always, 'Frank James knew who did it.' "

Cole knew his brother Bob's arm was broken at the elbow, but during their hasty retreat, he also learned Jim had been shot through the shoulder. Concern was for his brothers, not for the money they did not get at the fat bank in Northfield. They had been thwarted at other robberies, and as Frank James had once said, "We sometimes didn't get enough to buy oats for our horses. Most banks had very little money in them."

But this bank did and many, if not most, questions remained unanswered. Historians disagree as to who was really involved in the raid, which robbers were actually in the bank, and who pulled the fatal trigger. Jesse may have been in the bank for practical reasons. It was rumored he was not a good shot and he did not like shoot-outs. He had once fired six shots at a man and missed every time. Thus, he may have preferred being in the bank, rather than remaining in the street.

One historian believes both Bob Younger and Jesse James were in the bank. She feels Bob was usually placed outside, but since the Northfield affair was co-planned by him, he decided to be in the bank. If so, Bob would not have been drunk, his post would not have been changed to "protect" the others—the robbery would have instead been called off or a drunken person left out of it. The bandits would not have taken a chance; they were professionals.

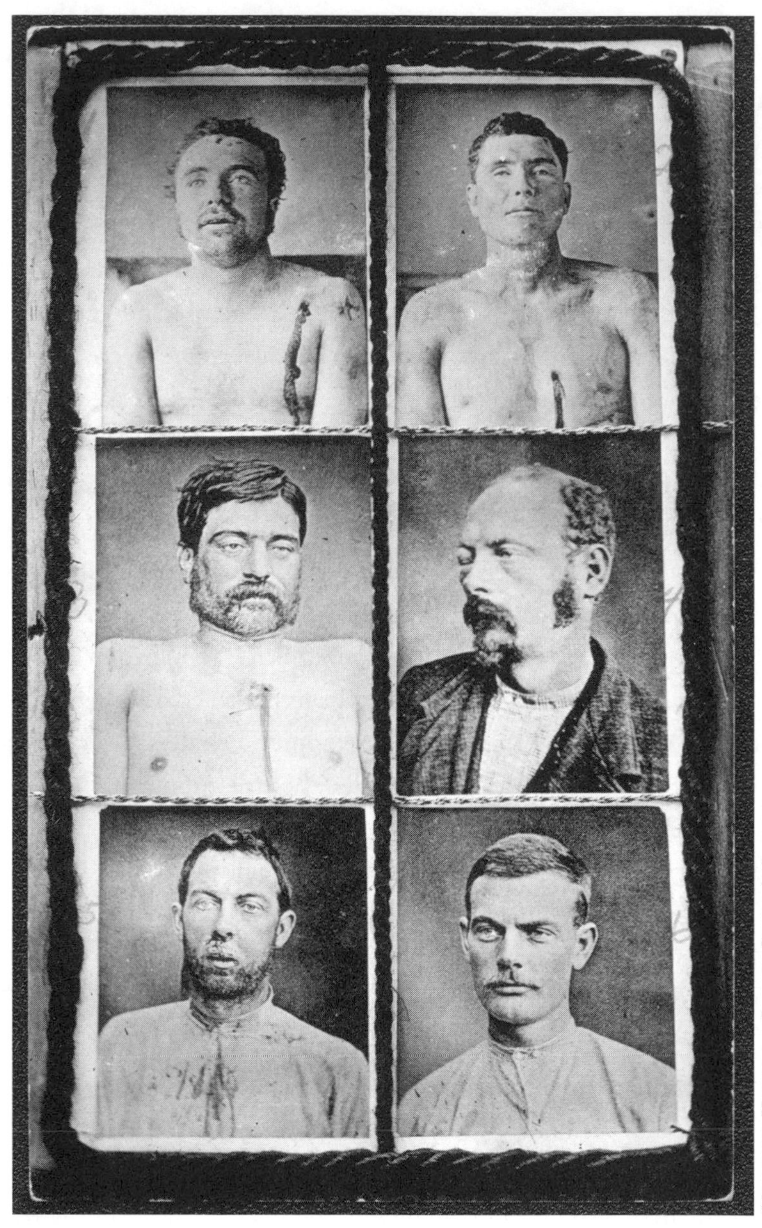

MINNESOTA HISTORICAL SOCIETY, SUMNER'S GALLERY

James-Younger gang members killed or captured at Northfield. Clockwise from upper left, Clell Miller, Bill Chadwell, Cole Younger, Bob Younger, Jim Younger, and Charlie Pitts.

Jesse perhaps went into the bank for the moral protection of Bob and because he felt he knew more about the situation. If Pitts went in, it would have meant that both Frank and Cole were left outside, which would not have agreed with the two leaders. Since Cole did not like to be in the banks, it was probably decided Frank would go in.

As this same scholar points out, it is curious indeed why Pitts was identified as being one of those in the bank. It was possible that one of the cashiers recognized Jesse (the only one who could probably be recognized) and was afraid of being a witness against him. Or, because of everyone being excited, it may have been a case of misidentification. Nor was Frank identified. If it were not for the many references to a dun horse, people would still be assuming it was Jesse who shot Heywood. If it were Jesse who shot Heywood, Cole would not have kept the secret of the rider of the dun horse as he did.

Although Pitts was well liked by his confederates, he may not have had the trust or prestige to be an inside man on such an important robbery. Of course, the egos of Frank and Cole would not have allowed them to both remain outside. And, since Bob was making such a big play of showing off his independence and importance, he probably would have strongly resisted Cole being in the bank.

Jim Younger once said: "The one time Bob listened to outside influences, firmly insisting that he was a man and could lead his own life, resulted in the Northfield affair. He was led to believe the subtly drawn picture by that master artist the crafty Mephistopheles, Jesse James, that there was a way of quick revenge on the North for our father's financial losses and the recovery of a huge sum of money. I never saw him so blindly enthused. Neither Cole or [sic] I could reach him. . . . Bob asked so many times if we forgave him for being so headstrong, both Cole and I assured him we were more at fault; being older, we should have found a way to prevent the whole thing."

Despite the horrible tragedy that crippled Northfield, and with the robbers still running free in their attempt to return to Missouri, the *Faribault Democrat* was able to inject some humor through one of its editorials: "The *Pioneer-Press and Tribune* has not yet charged directly that the Northfield bank robbers were led by Tilden [a presidential candidate] and Hendricks, but it says: 'Tilden lost two devoted followers when the brace of highwaymen fell dead at Northfield.' If the *Pioneer-Press* believes that it can make votes for Hayes by such vile and brutal insinuations as that, it has mistaken the temper of the people. It is expected in every issue of the *Pioneer-Press* to see that the robbers were Democratic Ku Klux engaged in the work of intimidating Republican voters. In its reports it constantly keeps before its readers the assertion that they were Democrats, and colors every circumstance with a partisan hue. But what else can be expected from the *Pioneer-Press*? It is quite as honorable as any of its campaign work."

In another section of the same issue of the *Faribault Democrat*, ran the following blurb: "The Northfield bank robbery is a sweet morsel to the *Pioneer-Press* who sees in it a chance to make votes for Hayes and Wheeler."

FROM

SPEECHES AND WRITINGS OF WM. H. WALLACE

By William H. Wallace

1914

So many different, and often contradictory, accounts have been written about the terrible disaster of the Jameses and the Youngers at Northfield, Minn., that the account given me by Liddil and obtained by him mainly, he said, from Jesse James, may be interesting. Of course Liddil at that time was not himself a member of the band. His account was as follows: The band was composed of eight men—Jesse James, Frank James, Clell Miller, Bill Chadwell, Cole Younger, Jim Younger, Bob Younger and Sam Wells. Wells is usually referred to in accounts of this robbery as "Charlie Pitts," but his true name was Sam Wells. I was raised in the same neighborhood with him, and knew him well. Liddil says these eight men started on horseback from the home of a well known citizen in the "Six Mile" country in Jackson County, whose name I need not give—he is now dead. Chadwell led them to Northfield, Minn., telling them that it was a new country and that there was a bank at Northfield where much money was kept on deposit. Heywood, the cashier, Liddil says,

Jesse James Farm & Museum, Kearney, Missouri

Jesse James achieved an early fame as an outlaw. Some people even felt it was an honor to be robbed by him, as evidenced by this early photo.

refused to open the vault of the bank. He crouched behind the counter, when Jesse James reached over and shot him, killing him. This gave the alarm. Some man, with a Winchester rifle, across the street, opened fire on the robbers. Clell Miller and Bill Chadwell were killed in front of the bank. Some of the others were wounded, their comrades carrying them away on their horses. As they departed from the town a Swede named Gustavason ran across the street and was shot and killed by the bandits. The whole country was aroused, and pursued the band. Bob Younger was so badly wounded that he could not travel. Liddil says it was proposed to kill him, and the balance of them make their escape, but Cole Younger would not hear to this. The James boys left by themselves, Cole, his brother, Jim, and Sam Wells staying with Bob. They were surrounded in the woods by their pursuers. A fight ensued. Sam Wells was killed, and Cole and Jim Younger wounded. All three of the Youngers were placed in the Minnesota penitentiary for life. Bob died in the penitentiary from his wounds, Jim and Cole being pardoned at the expiration of twenty-five years. According to Liddil's description, the escape of the James boys, one of whom was wounded, was beyond question one of the most remarkable feats in all history. They obtained an old wagon and team. The wounded man was placed in it, and they then drove down to Missouri, traveling sometimes in Iowa and sometimes in Nebraska and Missouri and Kansas until they reached the house of a friend, whom I need not mention, a few miles east of Kansas City, Mo. This friend took the wounded man in a wagon to Nashville, Tenn., the well brother going by train. While the Jameses lived at Nashville, as heretofore related, Frank James passed under the alias of "B. J. Woodson" and Jesse James under that of "J. B. Howard." So many different stories have been written about the attempted Northfield robbery that I thought I would give it just as Liddil gave it to me and just as I remember it was published in his confession after he gave himself up.

FROM

OZARK FOLKSONGS

Collected and Edited by Vance Randolph

1980

There are many old people in the Ozarks who knew the James and Younger boys very well indeed, and stories of their gallant deeds and unparalleled generosity are still current in our best hill-country families. Of Frank James in particular it is said that he never left a mountain cabin without placing a gold-piece on the "fire-board" to pay for his night's lodging, and some of his colleagues in derring-do were equally liberal. It is no wonder that the poverty-ridden hill-folk welcomed such men, concealed them when concealment was necessary, and helped them in every possible way.

There are no Jameses or Youngers in the Ozarks now, but something of the same attitude toward the highwayman still persists, and real outlaws are not altogether lacking even today. I remember a quiet, hard-faced young fellow whom one of my best friends introduced as his "cousin from out West," but it was not until several years later, when I had become more intimately associated with the family, that I learned his true identity. The fact that this man was a notorious criminal was kept from me at the time only because I was still regarded as a "furriner," and I discovered later that at least a dozen people in the neighborhood knew all about him.

There is no ballad about this man as yet, but one has only to talk with any of the local gossips to hear thrilling tales of his courage, generosity, kindness to women and children, and loyalty to those whom he regarded as his friends. Doubtless there is a grain of truth in every one of these narratives, but the touch of the troubadour is upon them all, and they are not reliable sources of definite information. So it is that Jesse James and Sam Bass and Cole Younger have already become semi-mythical heroes, and the material of the songs and stories about them is even now more legendary than historical.

Sung by Mrs. Lee Stephens, White Rock, Mo., Aug. 18, 1928.

Liv-in' in Mis-sou-ri was a bold bad man,
Known from Se-at-tle down to Bir-ming-ham,
From Den-ver Col-o-ra-do right a-cross the state,
From Bos-ton Mas-sa-chu-setts to the Gol-den Gate.

Some people will forget a lot of famous names,
But in every nick an' corner was a Jesse James,
We used to read about him in our home at night,
When the wind blew down the chimney we would shake with fright.

Jesse James said boys, some money we need,
Stepped out an' got his rifle an' his trusty steed,
An' then he galloped over for to see his brother Frank,
Says boys, we'll git the money from the Smithfield Bank.

Next mornin' when they arrived about ten o'clock,
The cashier of the bank he got an awful shock,
For Jesse had him covered with his forty-four,

An' he counted out half-a-million bonds or more.
Jesse he sat at home one day all alone,
His wife had left him there for to straighten out their home,
While scrubbin' out the kitchen the doorbell rang,
An' in stepped the leader of an outlaw gang.

Jesse says tonight before we make our haul
I'll just hang my dear wife's picture on the wall,
But a forty-four bullet went through Jesse's head,
An' the news went round the country that Jesse was dead.

Next week upon the tombstone was the words that ran,
If you want to be an outlaw be a single man,
For we all know Jesse wouldn't of lost his life,
If it hadn't been the picture of his darlin' wife.

From a manuscript sent me by Mrs. F. M. Warren, Jane, Mo., Feb. 25, 1927. Mrs. Warren writes: "We have had this ballet in the family for about forty years. I suppose it was written soon after Jessie was killed."

I suppose you all have heard
Of Bob and Charley Ford,
The slayers of pore Jessie James,
And how he was betrayed
Upon one April day
By the murders of Bob and Charley Ford.

Yes, Jessie leaves a wife
To mourn all her life,
A mother and two children so brave.
'Twas a dirty little coward
That shot Mister Howard
And laid Jessie James in his grave.

Saint Joe it was excited
As it never was before,
On hearing of pore Jessie's death.
And Bob and Charley Ford,
For the deeds they had did,
For protection to the citizens they fled.

The detectives held their breath
When they heard of Jessie's death,
And they wondered how he ever come to die.
For to get the big reward
It was Bob and Charley Ford
Shot pore Jessie James on the sly.

Jessie always was a friend
To all of the pore,
Although he had never suffered pain,
He and his brother Frank
They robbed the Northfield Bank,
And stopped the Glendale train.

Jessie he has gone down
To the Old Man's town,
Intending for to do as he pleased;
But he will rebel
In the city of Hell,
And maybe put old Satan to his knees.

Jessie James has gone to rest
With his hands upon his breast,
And there are many who never saw his face;
He was born one day in the county of Clay
And he came from the good old human race.

So it's now in the end
When cheated by a friend,
Just think of the days gone by;
And when you all drink
I hope you'll stop and think
How pore Jessie James come to die.

Pore Jessie leaves a wife
To mourn all her life,
And Frank is in the Independence jail,
But his friends stood by his side,
And they saw him through all right,
And give him any amount of bail.

FROM

FRONTIER DUST

By John Lord

1926

I went at the request of a neighbor as trail man to help him deliver thirty-six hundred head of cattle he had sold. When I got to his camp, I met the Thompson brothers. I thought I had never met two politer, pleasanter men. They received the cattle without a word of dispute as to ages or conditions. They paid for them with ready cash; they had it with them.

They drove the cattle into extreme southwestern New Mexico, an entirely unoccupied territory. They were there for about a year and a half unmolested when the Mexican ladrones made a raid across the Rio Grande and drove off a bunch of beef steers. The Thompsons' cowboys discovered the trail while it was still fresh, and the two Thompsons and their five cowboys followed it across the Rio Grande. The ladrones were regular cattle thieves who made a business of stealing cattle on both sides of the river and driving them to the mining camp in the Sierra Madras in the interior of Mexico and selling them for beef. After crossing back into Mexico, the ladrones picked up some Mexican cattle and were driving them along. The Thompson crowd overtook them before they got far from the river and they put up a fight. There were ten of the ladrones and seven of the Thompson crowd and they were all gun artists. They killed three of the Mexicans and the balance made a good getaway.

The Thompsons took all the cattle and started back for the Rio Grande. They had to camp one night before crossing the river, and they stopped at a ranch where they could get a corral for the cattle. The Mexicans happened to be having a dance that night, and the gringoes were asked to join in the dance. Mescal was plentiful. The Thompsons didn't drink at all but some of their men did. It wasn't long until some of the crowd were pretty well tanked up and when a man gets himself outside of enough mescal, he is ready to fight his grandmother's shadow or get up at two o'clock in the morning to pick his own pockets. Some of the gringoes paid too much attention to some of the senoritas, and the girls seemed to enjoy it too much to suit the greasers, until one of the greasers called down a gringo with a six-shooter. There were plenty ready to join in on both sides, so it soon became quite a pistol battle. The Mexicans got the worst of it. They stirred up trouble with the wrong bunch of Americans. There were two Mexicans dead and four badly wounded and only two Americans slightly wounded.

The Thompsons got out and drove to the Rio Grande as fast as they could make those cattle travel. They crossed the river without stopping to cut out the Mexican cattle and leave them behind. The Mexicans' cowboys soon discovered the trail crossing the river into the United States. The Thompsons did not mean to steal the Mexican cattle; they were in a hurry to get out of Mexico.

When the Mexican owners learned that some of their cattle had been driven into the United States by Americans and in so doing they had killed several citizens of Mexico and wounded several others, they took the matter up with our government without going to the trouble to learn the facts of the case, and charged the Thompsons with stealing cattle and killing Mexicans. Our government sent a deputy United States marshal to investigate. This marshal was born and raised in Independence, Missouri, and when he got to the Thompson brothers' ranch he found two of his old school fellows, Frank and Jesse James. They were the Thompson brothers. Frank and Jesse didn't do a thing that night but saddle up their two best horses and light out for parts unknown to the authorities. On investigation it was found that the Mexicans were at fault, and the matter was dropped. The James boys left everything in charge of their foreman and the public heard no more of them for over a year.

In the meantime the big silver boom at Leadville was at its highest, and I had gone there. One day after dinner I started for South Park to look after some freight teams I had on the road. I had to go south four miles to Malta, a stage station on the Arkansas River. There the road turned east down the river and crossed the Weston range out into South Park. This was the only stage road into Leadville and there were seventy-five to eighty-six horse concord stages each way every day, and oftentimes twenty-five or thirty of them would be traveling one right behind another. I got about half way to Malta when I saw two men coming to meet me. I said to myself, "If those aren't the Thompson brothers, I am badly fooled."

I was doing some fast thinking about them as to what they were up to, and what it was best for me to do. I knew then all about who the Thompson brothers were. I was sure they were up to some mischief and didn't want to be recognized by me or anyone else. I knew I didn't want to be recognized by them as I had no time to spend with the James boys. I expected to meet my teams that evening and ride back into Leadville early the next morning. So I made up my mind to do some acting and pretend I didn't know them and perhaps they wouldn't know me, as I was dressed as a cattle man when they saw me at the Chisholm's camp and now I was dressed as a miner. So I assumed the most innocent look I was capable of. When we met they said, "How do you do, sir?"

I said, "How are you, gentlemen?"

They asked me if I was in business in the camp. I said I was. They said they wanted to go into some business, not mining, as they didn't know anything about mining. They said they thought almost any business would pay where there was so much money in circulation as they had been told was in Leadville. While we were talking several stages passed, all heavily loaded with passengers, as all stages were, going in. They gave each other looks as the stages went by that made me suspicious that they might be figuring on the stages. They also gave each other looks that told me they knew me and thought I didn't know them. We talked about ten minutes and each went our way.

I expected to meet my wagons at the east foot of Weston range. I found them a day's drive beyond that place. The next morning as we were about ready to pull out of camp, the first stage passed coming out from Leadville. A man threw us a paper. Every one on the stage was yelling, "The James boys robbed twenty-four stages yesterday, half way between Leadville and Malta!" There is where Jesse said, "Keep your purse, lady, we are the James boys, we don't rob ladies." They didn't touch the mail and took no gold or silver, and had all the money they could carry.

I rode back to Leadville that morning and was shown where they robbed the stages. It was about a hundred and fifty yards south of where I met them, at a place where there were big rocks on each side of the road—no chance for a team to drive out and pass another. Frank took care of the driver of the first stage. That stopped and held all the balance until Jesse finished the job. They went from there to their camp in the Monte Cristo mountains, sixteen miles south of Malta, where they had several men and extra horses. Where they went from there the Lord only knows. All manner of deputy officers and posses scoured the surrounding mountains for days and found no trace of them except the location of their camp.

The public heard no more of the James boys until Bob Ford killed Jesse and Frank surrendered under an agreement with the governor of Missouri, a year or more after Bob Ford was killed.

I was in Trinidad, Colorado, when I met Jim Redd, a cattle man whose home was in Independence, Missouri. He said he had a friend who was starting a horse ranch in the Ozark Mountains in southwest Missouri, and he wanted three hundred head of two-year-old draft fillies.

"I am going home," he said, "and if you will come I am sure you can sell them to him."

I went. We got to Independence at night. The next morning Redd came to my hotel and told me his friend was out of town, would be home that evening late. We were walking up the main business street when Redd asked me if I knew that man sitting on that box, some distance from us. I said, "No." Just then the man got up. I said, "That is Frank James." He stepped in a cigar store and got a cigar, came out and sat down on the same box. Redd said, "Don't say anything, and see if he will recognize you." When we got about fifteen feet from him he threw up his head and looked at us, saying, "Hello, Lord, where did you come from? Do you know where I saw you last?"

I said, "I know where I saw you first and last."

He laughed and said, "Young man, you missed your calling; you should be on the stage. You are the best actor I ever saw. You are the only living man who completely fooled the James boys," and such a handshake I never had before or since.

We spent the day and night together until two o'clock next morning. He told me they didn't follow the business they did because they liked it, that they detested it. When the Civil War closed, on account of their being in Quantril's raid on Lawrence, Kansas, the United States government put a price on their heads, and to come in and surrender was simply sticking their heads into a halter, and they weren't built that way. So they made up their minds to play a game of sell out, and were obliged to do all this robbing to get money to hire people to hide them and lie for them. That was why the officers could never catch them.

I sold Redd's friend seventeen carloads of mares and went home.

FROM

THE JESSE JAMES POEMS

By Paulette Jiles

1988

Jesse Is Thrown Out of the New Hope Baptist Church

(Founding preacher, Reverend Robert James)

Minutes of the New Hope Baptist Church,
Kearney, Missouri August 12, 1876

The covenant of the New Hope Baptist Church
was called for and read.
A motion that the church get seven spittoons
for the use of the
congregation.
Carried.
It was requested Sister Dixie Thompson be
excluded from the church,

she being found guilty of dancing. Moved that the
        hand of fellowship
be withdrawn.
        Carried.
        Brother Elias Halloway confessed to having
        made a false impression
and requested forgiveness. He having made suitable
        amends, the question
was considered.
        Forgiveness voted.
        The case of Brother Jesse Woodson James
        being considered, charges
of revelry, robbery, murder, intemperance, and
        other un-Christian acts
being preferred, and he manifesting an impenitent
        spirit, motion that
the hand of fellowship be withdrawn and he be
        excluded from the church.
        Carried.
        On motion of Brother Hancock, Sister
        Georgina Williams to be excluded
from the fellowship of the church upon charges of
        walking disorderly
and having run off to join the Campbellites.
        Carried.
        After sermon by pastor, the doors of the church
        were opened to
membership. None responded.

        Clerk: J^{no} Burnett

FROM

A FRONTIER DOCTOR

By Henry F. Hoyt

1928

There was a famous Hot Springs six miles from Las Vegas, equipped with an old-time adobe line of bathhouses and a hotel. Scott Moore and his good wife were proprietors. Their cuisine was noted all through New Mexico and as they always had an extra fine dinner Sundays, there was, as a rule, a big crowd on that day.

I rode out one Sunday and found at a corner table the only vacant seat in the room. Glancing at the three guests already there, I was simply amazed to recognize the one on my left as Billy the Kid, urbane and smiling as ever. We shook hands, but neither mentioned a name.

We were chatting away of old times in Texas as if we were a couple of cowboy friends, when the man on Bonney's left made a comment on something he said. Whereupon Billy said, 'Hoyt, meet my friend Mr. Howard from Tennessee.'

The fourth man had nearly finished his meal when I sat down, and soon retired. Mr. Howard had noticeable characteristics. He had piercing steely blue eyes with a peculiar blink, and the tip of a finger on his left hand was missing. I mentally classed him as a railroad man. He proved to be most congenial, was a good talker, had evidently traveled quite a bit, and the meal passed pleasantly. After dinner we separated and Billy, taking me to his room, gave me, after pledging me to secrecy, one of the surprises of my life. Mr. Howard was no other than the bandit and train robber, Jesse James. I was skeptical, but Billy soon convinced me it was true. Jesse James had been in seclusion for some time; Mr. and Mrs. Moore were former friends whom he could trust, so he came out to size up the situation in a new territory. Billy also knew the Moores, and as he had not seen a passenger train since he was a youngster, he had slipped into Las Vegas, discarded his cowboy togs for an entire new city outfit of clothing, and was having the time of his life for a few days at the Hot Springs. He made his purchases at the store of Charley Ilfelt, who also knew him and who still remembers the incident. Mr. Ilfelt spent the winter of 1928-29 at the Hotel Virginia, Long Beach, California, and verified my recollection in regard to several incidents of the old days.

The Moores, finding themselves hosts of two of the most conspicuous outlaws the West has ever known, brought them together, and they apparently became friends.

Jesse James was prospecting and preparing to make a move, and after meeting Billy and sizing him up, made him a tentative proposition that they join forces and hit the trail together. Although both were outlaws with standing rewards for their capture, their lives and activities were entirely different. Billy was never a train or bank robber nor a hold-up man in any sense of the word. His only peculations had been rounding up cattle and horses carrying some one else's brand, a diversion more or less popular among many old-time cattlemen, and at that period not considered a crime—if one could get away with it. It was very much the same as bootlegging today.

His offenses, for which he was now an outcast, were entirely traceable to the now historic Lincoln County War. General Lew Wallace knew this or he certainly would never have made Billy the offer that will appear later.

On account of the difference in their status, and of the fact that a union with Jesse James would carry him away from the magnet at Fort Sumner, Billy turned down his proposal.

We all met again that evening and had quite a visit, 'Mr. Howard' little dreaming I knew his identity. Billy had said I was a doctor who had befriended him in the Panhandle. In discussing different parts of the country I could not resist the temptation to ask Mr. Howard if he had ever been at my old home, St. Paul, Minnesota. He replied in the negative, in the most nonchalant manner, and changed the subject. It was no doubt lucky for me that he was not a mind-reader. He evidently did not know of the recent publicity that had been given his former pal, Charley Pitts, and myself. It was a case of, 'where ignorance is bliss, 'twere folly to be wise.'

When I was alone with Billy, he gave me a brief account of his adventures after I left Tascosa. He had soon disposed of the few horses he had left, and with two of his party had returned to Lincoln County, by way of Bosque Redondo, of course, and found the war still on. If my memory is correct, Henry Brown and Fred Waite left him at Tascosa and traveled east. While at the Bosque, Billy had his picture taken and afterward made his Lolita a present of the watch and chain I had given him. He also told me that he had greatly improved his skill with a gun.

In Tascosa the rear of the store was a veritable graveyard for empty quart beer-bottles, and one of the outstanding sports of the cowboys was to set up six in a row and at a range of fifty yards shoot for the drinks, or whatever they might fancy, with their forty-fives. Here Billy was champion. He could pull his gun and demolish the six bottles in just one half the time of any one else. He and I exchanged weapons to see if there was any special magic in his, but it made no difference. He was also a marvelous shot with a Winchester.

In the picture of Billy the Kid can be seen the handle of his forty-five with which he had shot his way into fame—of a certain kind. The entire gun is shown in another picture with the profile of its present owner, that celebrated delineator of the old two-gun man of the Wild West, William S. Hart, of Newhall, California.

FROM

THE ROMANCE OF A WESTERN BOY: THE STORY OF CORSE PAYTON

By Gertrude Andrews

1901

Still on they went, the train clanking monotonously over the rails. Ahead the engine worked and puffed like some living creature. Its smoke blew back over the trail, at times enveloping the boys in its sooty embrace. Overhead the stars blinked, and the cool night air penetrated their thin summer clothing.

In the passenger cars behind people talked or slept all unconscious of any approaching danger.

By and by the boys saw lights flickering in the distance ahead. They were approaching a station. The train began to slacken up a trifle. Evidently they were going to stop. Now our two boys pricked up their ears and opened wide their eyes. Stops always meant danger. With a strained intentness they watched the car door, and held themselves ready to crouch at an instant's notice.

Then a most unexpected thing happened—a thing for which they were in no ways prepared. They had looked for the disturbers of their peace to come from the car, and never dreamed of anyone coming from another direction, any how not when the train was still in motion. But that is just what did happen. Out of the darkness beside the train there suddenly sprang a man who caught hold of the iron railing and deftly swung himself on to the car platform. He was a very big man, and behind him quickly followed another. Their appearance was so totally unexpected that the two boys, being taken so completely by surprise, had no time in which to crouch out of the way, and found themselves tangled in the men's legs before they could realize what had happened.

The men stumbled and caught themselves by the railing. There were several quick and energetic oaths, and the boys looked up to see something glisten in the dark, and felt the whiskey tainted breath of the men as they stooped to see what was in their way.

"It's a couple of kids stealing a ride," one of them said in a tone which suggested relief.

"What are you kids doing here?" the other asked hurriedly, "Come, get out of the way, or you'll get hurt."

And the next instant the two astonished lads found themselves sprawling in the weeds and grass growing along one side of the railroad track. How they got there they scarcely knew, the journey was made so quick. Hurt and dazed they pulled themselves up and looked after the train now slowing up to the station. Then, in mute accord, they started on a swift run. They would not be left out there alone without making a desperate effort to board the train again. They had learned to fight for their rights and not to accept defeat until no possible hope of success was left. They had seen some rough life with the circus.

On they rushed in hopes of being able to jump to another platform before the train should have begun to move on again. As they drew nearer, however, a sense of something unusual was felt by both. Over everything had spread such an ominous quiet. At the station was none of that usual bustle of railroad officials. In fact, the station seemed to be absolutely deserted. It was not a big station. They quickly discovered that.

Then a woman screamed and voices rose in angry altercation. There was swearing, quickly followed by the sound of scuffling. As yet the boys were not able to see what caused the trouble, but still they hurried on.

All at once a pistol shot rang out on the air. Some one groaned and fell heavily from a front car platform to the ground.

The boys stopped and grabbed each other in terror. With wide opened eyes they stood and stared at the train. Strange and horrible things were evidently going on there. From where they stood they could see the big bulk of a man filling up the door way in one end of the car. He moved back and they caught the bright flash of a revolver held in his hand. Through the car windows they could see men standing with arms raised above their heads, and dark shapes hurrying by them. They could hear women crying out in fright, and they felt the awful presence of that silent form lying deserted on the platform beyond.

The minutes were not many though ghastly long, before the man, who had evidently been guarding the car door, leaped to the ground and started towards the spot where stood our two white faced boys. They saw him coming and their hearts stopped beating. Instinctively they dropped to the ground, and, crouching in the grass, were hid by the night. Rapidly the man came towards them and then passed on into the darkness. In another instant they heard him talking in low hurried tones to some one whom they could not see. They recognized, also, the restless moving of horses. Before they could formulate any conjectures, however, four other men leaped from the train, and also came running in their direction. The boys clung tighter to each other and nearer to the earth. As the men pass them the boys could hear their heavy rapid breathing. Then off there in the darkness were some terse, muffled directions, and presently came the sound of horses' hoofs, and, then in another minute there was silence. Those five phantom shapes had vanished like five evil spirits.

But now people began swarming out of the train. Slowly the boys rose and cautiously approached it. A crowd had surrounded that silent form lying on the platform. Lanterns were brought. Men talked in nervous excited tones and women cried. Somebody called out:

"They've shot the conductor!"

"Is he dead?" several others asked.

A man, who was bending over the prostrate form, lifted his head and said something to those near to him, and what he said was passed on in low tones from one to another.

"Yes, he's dead."

"What place is this?" some one asked.

"Winston Junction," one of the men who carried a lantern made answer.

"Winston Junction," was repeated by several others.

"I wonder if it could have been the Jesse James gang?"

"That's probably who they were," the man with the lantern replied.

And it *was* the Jesse James gang. The next day people all over the country were reading the newspapers' exciting accounts of that famous hold-up at Winston Junction.

FROM

THE JAMES BOYS: A THRILLING STORY OF THE ADVENTURES AND EXPLOITS OF FRANK AND JESSE JAMES

Anonymous

circa 1882

Jesse James went with his wife and his two children to reside at St. Joseph, Mo., in November last, under the assumed name of Mr. Thomas Howard. He seemed to be living in security; but he was shadowed daily, and little dreamed that an avenging foe was so near.

Two young men, assuming the name of Johnson, but whose real names are Robert and Charles Ford, the former 20 years of age, the latter 24, who hailed from Richmond, Ray County, Mo., and who are said to be cousins to Jesse James by marriage, were detailed by Governor Crittenden, H. H. Craig, Police Commissioner of Kansas City, and Sheriff Timberlake of Clay County, to make sure of Jesse at all risks and hazards.

The Ford boys were no strangers to either Frank or Jesse. Their home in Richmond has often been the stopping place of the James Gang. If these boys had not been actual accomplices with Frank and Jesse in their lawless exploits, they had evinced so much sympathy with them, that there could be nothing remarkable in their assumed desire to join the band of robbers. No man is at all times wise, and the most cautious men are sometimes caught napping when their interests need them to be widest awake.

When Jesse, with his wife and "twa wee bairns" came to live in St. Joseph, they lived in the southeast part of the city, on the hill not far from Worth's Hotel. The winter months passed very quietly, and Jesse was but very seldom seen. He was in the habit of keeping close indoors during the day, and all the visits made to the city were paid after nightfall; and then the journey was short and the return home was speedy. The nightly errand was for his favorite journals, the Chicago *Tribune*, the Cincinnati *Commercial* and the Kansas City *Times;* in the perusal of which he spent most of his time. The neighbors took little interest in the new family. If they said anything at all, it was to the effect that the "Howard's" were a very quiet people.

Christmas passed pleasantly. Jesse had the reputation of being a very devoted father, and when he had no "professional business" on hand, he would spend most of his time in "cutting up with the young 'uns." Everything indicates that had Jesse chosen a quiet and honorable walk in life, he would have been a thoroughly domestic man.

All through the history of the James' Boys there has been a remarkable exhibition of filial affection. Frank and Jesse have never failed to show strong affection for their mother, while Mrs. Samuels, though stern and unbending in her nature, evinced boundless love for her sons, and was undoubtedly proud of their terrible exploits. She had been a faithful ally many and many a time. She had often obtained information of the greatest importance to them in their wild expeditions; and if half that is said of her is true, she was frequently consulted, and her counsel taken in the plots and schemes of the robber band.

About a fortnight before his death Jesse paid his last visit to his mother, at the Kearney homestead. The Spring was just making its appearance, and the old home of his childhood was donning its robe of

Jesse James Farm & Museum, Kearney, Missouri

The wife of Jesse James, Zerelda, with their son, Jesse Edwards James, and daughter, Mary Susan James, in a photo taken circa 1882.

vernal beauty. Little did Jesse think that before the bud changed to blossom he would lie sleeping under the grass with a bullet through his brain. His life had always been in danger. He had been in more "imminent perils" than Othello could recount. But this time did not seem especially perilous, except from hints that came of the thorough determination of Governor Crittenden to make a full end of bank robbing and train wrecking. The arrest of so many confederates had somewhat unnerved him. And Dick Little's surrender was ominous. But, like Hamlet in the play, he "defied augury." He had borne a charmed life so far, and he would not blench with fear till there was some real cause.

Of the details of that last visit into Clay County only little is known; but that little is of great import to this narrative. It was during this visit that Robert Ford made the final arrangements that ended so disastrously for Jesse. Nearly all Jesse's old comrades were in prison or dead. The James Gang was utterly broken up, and Jesse evidently had no intention of giving up his course of life. What he wanted was new and good material. And Robert Ford seemed to him the kind of stuff to make a bank robber out of. And probably Jesse was right in his estimate of his dear relative.

Another matter was pressing on Jesse's attention; funds were getting low. He had not more than some $600 or $700, and the failing coffers must be replenished. The enormous amounts of money obtained by this Gang is only a little more remarkable than the speed with which it disappeared. It is another illustration of the old adage, "easy come, easy go."

A reference to the earlier pages of this book will show that the James Brothers must have secured by their nefarious proceedings not less than $275,000; and yet, Jesse James had not a thousand dollars when he died.

At this last visit home, Jesse talked over a plot with Robert Ford for robbing another bank. But all unknown and unsuspected, he was himself the victim of a plot within a plot. Deep and subtle and far-seeing as he was

"Beneath his depth,
A deeper depth
Lay threatening to devour."

PART III

AND LAID POOR JESSE IN HIS GRAVE

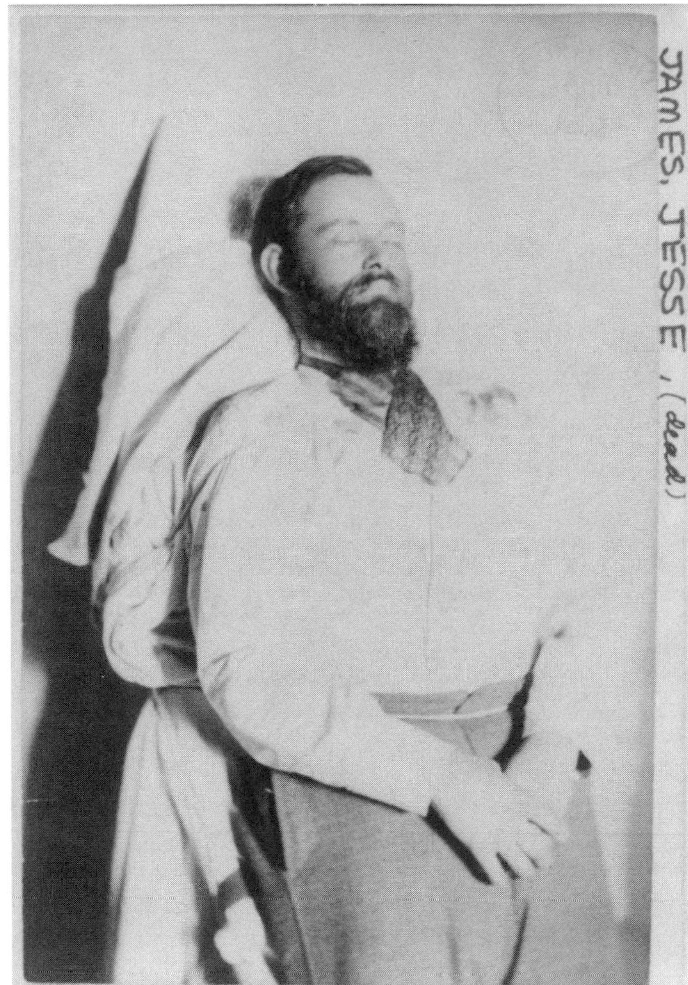

Library of Congress, LC-USZ62-42551

Jesse James, posed in death at age thirty-four.

An occasion startling enough to etch itself into our collective memory, the death of Jesse James at the hands of Robert Ford became a profound moment in American history. Among those who have written about the event in verse, essays, letters, and fiction, there are names as diverse as Paulette Jiles, John Edward Hicks, and Pulitzer prize winner MacKinlay Kantor. We've excerpted the work of these writers, as well as an account from one of the newspapers of the day. The known events inside the house have been very ably reconstructed by William Settle.

Robert Ford pled guilty to murder, was pardoned by Missouri Governor Crittenden, and went off to his own ignoble demise, largely despised by history. Meanwhile, the mythology of Jesse James has not only survived, it has prospered. A cultural icon that continues to work his way into novels and movies, the formula of Robin Hood meeting his death by betrayal has proven too tempting to resist.

— Harold Dellinger

FROM

JESSE JAMES WAS HIS NAME: OR, FACT AND FICTION CONCERNING THE CAREERS OF THE NORTORIOUS JAMES BROTHERS OF MISSOURI

By William A. Settle Jr.

1966

The frequency and diversity of reports concerning the whereabouts and doings of the James brothers throughout 1881 provoked the editor of the Liberty *Tribune* to comment that "the Irishman's axiom, that nothing except a flea can occupy two places at the same time, will have to be enlarged to include the James boys." But tangible evidence that the James band was rendezvousing in Kentucky caused officials to make extensive raids in Logan and Nelson counties of that state in late October and early November. No members of the band were captured, but there was little doubt that they frequently visited relatives and old guerrilla friends there.

One Kentuckian reportedly said he regretted that the raids had not netted the outlaws. However, he expressed what was probably the typical viewpoint of people in that section when he added: "Personally, we have no desire whatever to take in the reward offered for their capture, unless we could purchase their bodies on credit and ship them C.O.D. to Missouri."

In February, 1882, another foray of officers into Kentucky was more successful, and Clarence Hite, cousin of Jesse James, was arrested and returned to Missouri. He entered a plea of guilty to participation in the robbery at Winston on July 15, 1881, and was sentenced to twenty-five years in prison. Reports varied as to whether he had implicated other members of the band in a confession, and mystery surrounded the handling of the case. The public, possessing little information, wondered why he had pleaded guilty instead of standing trial.

In the last days of March, the farm boys arrested after the robbery at Blue Cut in September, 1881—Creed Chapman, John Bugler, and John Mott—came to trial at Independence. John Land, the member of the gang who had confessed and on whose statements Prosecuting Attorney Wallace was depending for conviction, testified that the boys had joined older members of a band led by Jesse James and Dick Liddil. They had not shared in the loot, for Jesse had taken it all, with the promise, never fulfilled, to divide it later. The case against these men was not completed, for Wallace decided that Land's confession was a fake. He entered a nolle prosequi in the case on April 6, for other happenings had interrupted the trial.

On March 31 the press announced that Dick Liddil had surrendered, and in time the details relating to his action came to general knowledge. Following the trial of Ryan in September, 1881, Liddil had become apprehensive that Jesse James suspected him of planning to give evidence for the state as Tucker Bassham had done. Ed Miller had disappeared, and there were indications that Jesse had killed him. Fearing Jesse, Liddil left him. Soon he was at the Ray County home of Mrs. Martha Bolton, sister to Charles and Robert Ford. Robert Woodson (Wood) Hite, brother of Clarence Hite and cousin of Jesse James, who Bassham had testified was a member of Jesse's band, appeared at Mrs.

Bolton's also. An argument started, and in the resulting fight Robert Ford and Dick Liddil killed Wood Hite. The real trouble between Hite and Liddil seemed to be rivalry for Martha Bolton's favors. Wood's body was moved upstairs, where it lay for a day, and then at night it was taken out and buried, wrapped in a horse blanket.

Liddil now knew that he might have to answer to both the law and Jesse James for the murder of Wood Hite, so he decided to turn state's witness. First, he sent Mattie Collins, his wife or mistress, to W. H. Wallace, who promised that there would be no prosecution against him in Jackson County if he gave himself up and assisted the officers by furnishing information that would result in the arrest of other members of the band. Since Wallace could guarantee nothing beyond immunity in Jackson County, a woman believed to be Martha Bolton visited Governor Crittenden, veiled so that he did not know her identity, and sought pardons for members of the James band.

As a result of this interview Liddil surrendered to Sheriff James H. Timberlake of Clay County on January 24. With information obtained from Liddil, officers were at work to complete the breakup of the band. Those most active were Sheriff Timberlake, Kansas City Police Commissioner Henry H. Craig, and Governor Crittenden.

When the news broke that Liddil had surrendered, Crittenden issued a public statement to the effect that before the surrender he had had an interview with a lady, whom he did not know at the time, but with whom he had since become acquainted. He declined to promise pardons for the bandits in advance of their surrender, but did agree to use his influence to prevent punishment of any member of the band, except Frank and Jesse James, who would voluntarily surrender, make a full confession, and give information concerning the whereabouts of others.

Clarence Hite's plea of guilt was no longer a mystery. Confronted by Liddil, he had chosen to accept a twenty-five-year sentence rather than stand trial. On April 3, 1882, with excitement still high over announcement of Liddil's surrender, dispatches from St. Joseph, Missouri, flashed the news that Jesse James was dead. His death had been reported falsely so often that many afternoon papers which received the brief message in time for their last edition warned readers to await confirmation. But the news was true this time! Almost as startling was the information that Jesse James, under the name of Thomas Howard, had lived in St. Joseph since November, 1881, with his wife and two children, and for the six months preceding the move to St. Joseph, the period in which the robberies at Winston and Blue Cut had occurred, the family had resided in Kansas City, where Jesse was known as J. T. Jackson.

Charles and Robert Ford, newly recruited, youthful members of the band, had been staying with Jesse and his family for several days. Charles had helped rob the Chicago and Alton train in September, 1881, but Bob had not yet participated in a robbery; plans were being made for the robbery of a bank in Platte City on April 4. Bob, however, had been in contact with Crittenden, Timberlake, and Craig for several weeks and through his older brother had gained Jesse's confidence. After breakfast on the morning of Monday, April 3, the three men went into the living room. Jesse removed his guns, laid them on a bed, and stepped up on a chair to straighten and dust a picture. Catching him thus off guard, Bob quickly drew his pistol and shot his host in the back of the head. Jesse fell lifeless to the floor.

Zee rushed into the room and, on seeing her husband lying dead, gave way to unrestrained grief and anger. As quickly as they could escape the house, the Ford brothers telegraphed Governor Crittenden, Timberlake, and Craig that they had killed their man and gave themselves up to the St. Joseph authorities. When townspeople appeared at the house, Zee first maintained that the dead man was Thomas Howard, but she soon broke down and revealed that he was indeed Jesse James. St. Joseph forgot the heated city election of the day, and the curious swarmed to the little house to view the murdered outlaw's body.

Doubt existed as to whether the dead man was really Jesse James, so identification of the body was the first important task to be performed. The grief of Jesse's wife Zee and of Mrs. Samuel, who arrived early the next morning, seemed so genuine and Mrs. Samuel's condemnation of the murderers so bitter and characteristic of her that those who observed the women were convinced that the body was Jesse James's.

Timberlake, Craig, and Wallace went to St. Joseph. Timberlake had known Jesse years before, having seen him last in 1870, and he recognized the body as that of his former acquaintance. Wallace took with him a Clay County farmer, William Clay, two former guerrilla associates of the James brothers, Harrison Trow and James Wilkerson, and Mattie Collins. They all identified the body as that of Jesse James, to Wallace's satisfaction. Photographs showed two scars from bad wounds on the right side of the chest, and the newspaper accounts pointed out that the tip of the middle finger of the left hand was missing and that there were scars from other wounds on the body. These wounds had long been part of the James legend.

Some were skeptical, however, and believed that a hoax was being perpetrated. This group was small. Countless others who claimed to know Jesse viewed the body, and no general opinion arose that the body was not his. The coroner's jury reached the verdict: "We the jury find that the deceased is Jesse James, and that he came to his death by a shot from a pistol in the hands of Robert Ford."

The gold watch worn by Jesse when he was killed was returned to its owner, John A. Burbank of Richmond, Indiana, who had lost it and a diamond stickpin in the stage robbery at Hot Springs in January, 1874. Other valuables that were identified as property of victims of robberies attributed to the James band were found in Jesse's possession. Horses and saddles in Jesse's stable had been stolen in northwest Missouri in recent weeks, but Jesse's friends charged the Ford boys with their theft. Many items found at the James house in St. Joseph were confiscated by officials and were then recovered by their rightful owners. Among the things unclaimed and later returned to Mrs. James was a copy of *Noted Guerrillas*, John N. Edwards' book-length defense of the Jameses and their fellows.

It was necessary for Governor Crittenden to ask that the body be turned over to Mrs. James before the St. Joseph officials would surrender it. Then a special train provided by the Hannibal and St. Joseph Railroad took the funeral party to Kearney, where hundreds of old acquaintances, friends of the family, and curiosity seekers viewed the corpse and attended the funeral. The Reverend R. H. Jones of Lathrop, Missouri, read from the Book of Job, beginning with "Man that is born of a woman is of few days, and full of trouble," and the fourth and fifth verses of the Thirty-ninth Psalm, which include the words, "Lord make me to know mine end." Matthew 24:44, "Therefore be ye also ready; for in such an hour as ye think not, the Son of Man cometh," was the text the Reverend J. M. Martin of Kearney used for the funeral sermon. His discourse offered comfort to the family through faith in God and made the sudden, unexpected death of Jesse a warning to sinners. From the little church in Kearney the body was taken to the Samuel home and interred in a deep grave in the yard, beneath a huge coffee bean tree.

The dramatic figure in these events was Mrs. Samuel, who gave vent to her grief and heaped curses upon the traitors who caused Jesse's death. When asked at the inquest if the dead man were her son, she replied that he was, but, "Would to God that it were not!" Upon meeting Dick Liddil as she left the inquest, she pointed an accusing finger at him and exclaimed, "Traitor! traitor! traitor! God will send vengeance on you for this; you are the cause of all this. Oh, you villain; I would rather be in my boy's place than in yours!" When the funeral party reached Kearney she cried out to Sheriff Timberlake, "Oh, Mr. Timberlake, my son has gone to God, but his friends still live and will have revenge on those who murdered him for money."

Crittenden, Timberlake, and Craig denied that they knew of Jesse's presence in St. Joseph and of Ford's intention to murder him, although they admitted that they knew Ford was with Jesse and intended to betray him. Further, Bob Ford made a statement that exonerated them. Whatever the arrangement with Ford, Governor Crittenden stood by the two brothers. A grand jury at St. Joseph indicted them for murder in the first degree. On April 17, they entered pleas of guilty, and were sentenced to be hanged. Crittenden received the news of the sentence by telegraph and that afternoon granted them a full and unconditional pardon.

Was it the prospect of the reward that had motivated Bob Ford to kill Jesse James? Probably. How much reward did he get? Governor Crittenden boasted in his autobiography that "the proclamation of a reward accomplished its purpose in less than one year at a cost not exceeding $20,000, not one cent of which was drawn from the state." However, he never revealed to whom the reward money was paid, other than the Fords, nor is it known how much they received. A part of the total undoubtedly went to those who apprehended Ryan and Hite. Some believed that Crittenden himself took part of the fund provided by the railroads, that others like Craig and Timberlake got a share, and that the Ford brothers' part was meager. The search for the true story of the distribution of the reward is one of the elusive, but intriguing, pursuits of students of the James legend.

If the newspapers are to be believed, Crittenden, in his desire to get the credit for the killing of Jesse James, showed poor judgment. The *Post-Dispatch* quoted him as telling a reporter after the killing: "People have no idea how much trouble I have had in getting *my* men to work together and keep at it. *My* great point in the whole business has been secrecy. *My* success has been entirely brought about by keeping quiet and not revealing *my* information before I had effected *my* purpose." He also boasted that he had no excuse or apology to render for his part in the affair, and he expressed the belief that the Fords deserved credit, not abuse, for the assassination.

FROM

THE SECRET LIFE OF JESSE JAMES

By Arthur Winfield Knight

1996

St. Joseph
Monday, March 27, 1882

Dear Susan,

You know how Ma can be. She gets an idea in her head and she won't let go of it. I was visiting her and the family with Bob and Charley Ford last weekend when Ma pulled me aside.

It was twilight and the sky looked like a bloody rose, getting redder and redder. I thought it was going to burst into flame, the clouds shriveling up like burning petals, but the light just gradually faded, the way our lives do.

Ma said, "I don't like that boy."

"You just don't know Bob."

"I don't know any snakes, either, but I know enough not to lie down next to one so it can bite me."

"You've never liked anyone I've known. Cole was too bawdy. Zee wasn't good enough."

"Trust your family," Ma continued. "That's all you can trust."

"Zee *was* family."

"Well, that just proves what I'm saying. Look at how she's turned out. She's stood by you."

I paused, tired. The two of us sat on the rockers on the front porch. Rocking together. It made a kind of music. Lulling. I remembered the way I used to rock Mary's bassinet. Back and forth, back and forth. It's one normal thing I've done.

"For what it's worth, Zee doesn't like Bob either. But she doesn't know why. I've asked her to be specific, to give me even one reason, but she can't."

"Women *feel* things," Ma said. "They have intuition."

Ma and Zee believe in omens. They can see death in the bottom of a tea cup. All I can see are some soggy leaves.

"Then why didn't you know the Pinkertons were going to throw that bomb into our house?"

I could see the tears welling up in her eyes in the twilight, but she held them back. Back. She never could show much emotion, at least to me. Sometimes I thought I was an accident. That Frank was the one she really loved.

Ma said, "Don't you ever talk to me like that again. Ever."

I stopped rocking and walked to the edge of the porch. It was almost dark now, but I could see the lantern burning in the barn. Charley and Bob were out there with the horses. They were always off someplace together.

"I didn't come here to argue, Ma. I just wanted to see you."

She came up behind me. I could hear the boards squeaking under her feet, but I didn't turn around. Then I felt her hand on my shoulder, and I remembered the way she'd knead my shoulders when she still had both hands, before the Pinkertons blew one of them off with their damn bomb.

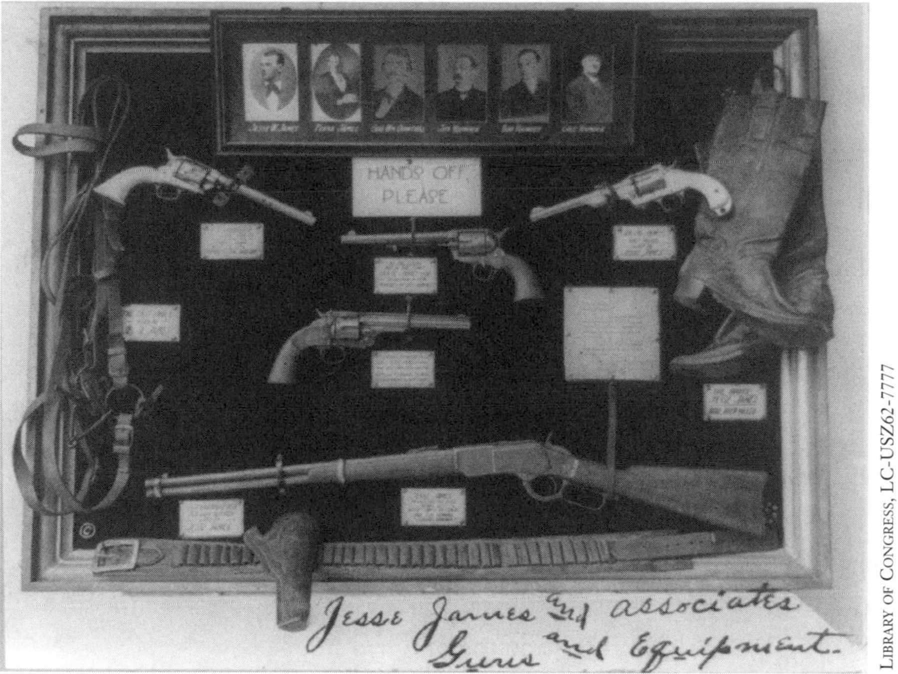

LIBRARY OF CONGRESS, LC-USZ62-7777

The aura of Jesse James and his gang extended even to the boots they might have worn and the horse reins they could have used. This photo was taken circa 1921.

"I just don't want them to get you," Ma said. "It seems like everyone I know is dyin' off."

"I'm not going to die . . . yet."

"I pray for you . . . nightly."

"I need all the help I can get," I told Ma, "divine or otherwise." I gave her a quick hug and said, "If I never see you here again, I'll see you in Heaven," then I walked toward the barn to saddle up. I must have crossed that yard thousands of times—crying, laughing, lonely, on the run—in the more than thirty years I've been alive.

When Bob, Charley and I rode off, the sky looked like a giant piece of wrinkled canvas. There weren't any stars and lightning cut the sky in two.

The rain hit hard by the time we were about thirty miles from St.

Joseph and we tied our horses in front of a small church we came to. We went inside, shaking the water off our slickers, and Bob said, "I hate this goddamn rain."

"You shouldn't take the Lord's name in vain," I said.

"That sounds funny, coming from you."

"Why?" I went to the altar and lit some of the candles. Outside, the lightning flashed faster than you could blink. Thunder shook the church.

"Because of the men you've killed," Bob said.

"They all deserved it."

"I wonder if they looked at it like that? Or their families?"

"I don't care how they look at it." I lay down on one of the pews but felt funny about it, so I sat on the floor, leaning against the wall beneath a stained glass window. When the lightning flashed, the shadow of the Cross stretched out in front of me. I closed my eyes for what I thought was a few seconds but I must have fallen asleep because when I opened them again, it was morning and the rain had stopped.

I went outside, walking through the muddy little graveyard beside the church. One of the tombstones said GONE ON TO GREATNESS and I thought about little Archie, resting in the shade of the juniper tree in the Mt. Olivet Cemetery. His tombstone says KILLED BY A BOMB.

I wondered what my epitaph would be but I got depressed thinking about that so I went back into the church. Nudging Charley and Bob with the toe of my boot, I said, "We'd better get riding."

Jesse

St. Joseph
Sunday, April 2, 1882

Dear Frank,

The wind's blowing from the south-east and it's raining. I pay a lot of attention to the weather because I don't have much else to do.

The temperature is 44 degrees and the sun rose at 6:10. I've sat around here doing nothing for so long. I'm beginning to feel rusty.

The barometer reads 30-74.

Miss Sara Bernhardt is getting married in London tomorrow. I hate myself for doing nothing.

I read the papers or pretend to read the papers. I spend hours sitting and staring. I buy the morning and the evening news. It's all the same.

I keep telling myself to do something, even if it's wrong. I've made mistakes before and survived them, although surviving doesn't seem as important as it used to. A man needs a reason to be alive.

Maybe my luck will change if I do one more job. Bob and I have been looking at a bank in Platte City. This Tuesday there's going to be a sensational murder trial going on there. Bob and I could be in and out of the bank in minutes and Charley could hold the horses and serve as our lookout. There must be a hundred thousand dollars just sitting there . . . waiting for us . . . and it would be a three way split.

Do something. Even if it's wrong.

We can't go on like this. Even the children are restless. They know something isn't right. Last night at dinner little Jesse asked Bob, "Why are you always here?"

Bob just looked at his plate, hard, and bunched up his napkin.

"I liked it better when you didn't eat with us all the time."

"Stop that," Zee said. "You apologize to your Uncle Bob."

"He isn't my uncle. He isn't. Why is he always here?" His voice broke and Mary began to cry and Zee said, "Why is it we can never have a peaceful meal anymore?" Then she took the kids to their room and I got up from the table, nodding at Bob.

"I don't seem to be very hungry," I said. I sat down with the paper in the next room but I didn't look at it.

Bob came to the door and said, "If you'd like me to leave—"

"No, it's all right."

"I think I'll go out for a beer. Do you want to join me?"

"You go ahead, Bob."

I don't know why we'd had him live with us. I guess it gives me someone to talk to now that you're gone. I'm away from everyone I love—Ma, you, Susan—except Zee. Bob's like a dog. You could kick him and he'd wag his tail.

I get so lonely . . . Sometimes I'll just sit here, oiling my pistol and wiping it down. Counting the number of shells I have left. Sometimes I think that's about all I have left: bullets.

When I tucked my son into bed I told him, "You shouldn't have said that to Bob."

"I don't like him being here, Pa."

"He'll be going . . . soon. Try to be patient. To understand."

"I love you."

"I love you, too."

Then I hugged him and kissed Mary and turned the lantern down. I didn't turn it off because they're afraid of the dark now.

There's a fine mist out as I walk down the hill toward where the Pony Express used to be. It's been more than twenty years. They claim they could have galloped around the world twenty-four times in the year and a half they existed. And now the stables are boarded up and weeds are growing through the cracks in the cobblestones out front. I stand there, trying to bring it all back: the smell of the horses and the hay and the men sweating, but it's all gone. Gone.

The rain has almost stopped as I head back up the hill. The old pain is back in my chest and I know I'll have to take some morphine by the time I get home. And there's the pain behind my eyes. And the other pain.

I can almost hear my heart beating as I walk up the hill and I begin to sweat. By the time I reach our house I'm bathed in perspiration.

Zee says, "You shouldn't have gone out in the rain. You'll catch pneumonia."

I mix the morphine and water, shivering. *To everything there is a season, and a time to every purpose under the heaven. A time to be born, a time to die.* I take the morphine without answering Zee.

Finally, I say, "We all have to die from something," then I sink into a chair, waiting for it to be light.

Jesse

"Judgment For Jesse," *St. Joseph Western News*, April 7, 1882

When we approached the door leading into the front room on Monday morning, our eyes beheld a man lying on the floor, cold in death with the blood still oozing from his wound. Walking into the room and around the dead man's body, we opened the door leading into a kitchen where we found a woman with two small children, a boy and a girl.

At first the woman refused to say anything about the shooting but after a time she said "the boys" who had killed her husband had been living with them for some time and their name was Ford. Charles, she said, was a nephew, but she had never seen the other, Robert, until he came to the house with her husband a few weeks ago. When asked what her husband's name was, she said it was Howard.

When we asked her when the shooting was done she said, "I had been in the kitchen and Charles had been helping me all morning. He entered the front room and about three minutes later I heard the report of a pistol. Upon opening the door I discovered my husband lying in his own blood.

"I ran to the front door as Charles was getting over the fence, but Robert was standing in the front yard with a pistol in his right hand."

At this juncture the Ford boys made their appearance and gave themselves up to the officers and told them the man they had killed was Jesse James and now they claimed the reward. They said, "We feel proud we killed a man who is known all over the world as the most notorious outlaw who ever lived."

After breakfast, Jesse and the Ford boys had gone into the living room. Jesse took off his pistols, stepping up on a chair to dust a picture. When he did, Bob drew his pistol, shooting Jesse in the back of the head from about four feet away.

The marshal then asked the woman calling herself Mrs. Howard if what the Ford boys had said was true.

Screaming at the top of her lungs she called them cowards and asked, "Why did you kill the one who had always befriended you?"

The marshal said, "They claim they killed him to get the reward money," then he led her from the room.

Holding her little children to her bosom she said, "I cannot shield them much longer. Even after the Fords shot my husband who has been trying to live a peaceful life, I tried to withhold his name. But it is true. My husband is Jesse James and a kinder hearted and truer man to his family never lived."

This confession from the wife of the most notorious outlaw who ever lived created a profound sensation in the room. The thought that Jesse James had lived for six months within our city and walked our streets daily caused one to shudder with fear.

When the wife made her confession, we begged her to tell us about Jesse, Frank and the Ford brothers and she said she would. "The deed is done. Why should I keep quiet any longer? Charlie and Robert Ford have been here with my husband and while I never trusted them, little did I think they would kill him."

Jesse's body was neatly clad in a business suit of cashmere, of a dark brown substance which fit him very neatly. He wore a shirt of spotless whiteness, with collar and cravat, and looked more the picture of a staid businessman than the outlaw that he was.

The most renowned robber of his age, Jesse quickly rose to eminence in his gallant and dangerous profession and his exploits excited the emulation of small boys. Jesse was cut off in the prime of his strength and beauty, not by the hands of the hangman but by the shot of a base assassin of whom the Governor of the State of Missouri was the accomplice.

Two days after Jesse was murdered, he was buried at the James farm in Kearney. The Reverend R. H. Jones of Lathrop read from the Book of Job: "Man that is born of a woman is of few days, and full of trouble." And the Reverend J. M. Martin of Kearney read a text from Matthew:

"Therefore be ye also ready; for in such an hour as ye think not, the Son of Man cometh."

Because Mrs. Samuel feared her son's grave would be desecrated by souvenir hunters, Jesse James was buried in an especially deep grave. As his casket was lowered into the ground, hundreds of mourners—relatives, friends, clergy and even officers of the law—united in paying extraordinary honors to Jesse's memory.

Go thou and do likewise.

FROM

THE *KANSAS CITY DAILY JOURNAL*

1882

GOOD BYE, JESSE!

The Notorious Outlaw and Bandit, Jesse James,
Killed at St. Joseph

BY R. FORD, OF RAY COUNTY,

A Young Man but Twenty-one Years of Age.

THE DEADLY WEAPON USED

Presented to His Slayer by His Victim but a Short Time Since.

A ROBBERY CONTEMPLATED

Of a Bank at Platte City—To Have Taken Place Last Night.

JESSE IN KANSAS CITY

During the Past Year and Residing on One of the Principal Streets.

KANSAS CITY EXCITED

Over the Receipt of the News—
Talks with People—Life of the Dead Man.

"I've got him, sure," was the telegram that came to the city yesterday. It was meaningless to almost everybody, yet it contained news of the greatest importance. Jesse James was the person referred to, and as he was a corpse, the sender of the dispatch was confident that he had him, sure.

At 9 o'clock yesterday morning the notorious outlaw was shot dead, at St. Joseph, Mo., by Robert Ford, a young man about 21 years of age, from Ray county. Ford, being acquainted with the James gang, recently planned the death of Jesse. This plan was concocted in this city, and was, as it has been seen, successfully carried out. His brother Charles was with him at the time of the killing, and the wife of Jesse was in the kitchen of the house in which they were living. At his death Jesse was hanging pictures. He had but a few moments before being killed divested himself of his coat and his revolvers. He never spoke a word after falling to the floor. The slayers gave themselves up soon after the killing, and an inquest over the remains was begun.

THE KILLING IN DETAIL

Special Dispatch to the Kansas City Journal.

ST. JOSEPH, MO., April 3.—Between 8 and 9 o'clock this morning Jesse James, the Missouri outlaw, before whose record the deeds of Fra Diavolo, Dick Turpin and Shinterhannes dwindle into insignificance, was killed by a boy 21 years old named Robt. Ford, at his temporary residence on Thirteenth and Lafayette streets, in this city. In the light of all moral reasoning the shooting was wholly unjustifiable, but the law is vindicated, and the $50,000 reward offered by the state for the body of the brigand dead or alive will doubtless go to the man who had the courage to draw a revolver on the notorious outlaw when his back was turned, as in this case. There is little doubt that the killing was the result of a premeditated plan formed by Robert and Charles Ford several months ago. Charles had been an accomplice of Jesse James since the 3d of last November, and entirely possessed his confidence. Robert Ford, his brother, joined Jesse near Mrs. Samuels (the mother of the James boys) last Friday a week ago, and accompanied Jesse and Charles to this city Sunday, March 23.

Jesse, his wife and two children removed from Kansas City (where they had lived several months until they feared their whereabouts would be suspected) to this city, arriving here November 8, 1881, coming in a wagon and accompanied by Charles Ford. They rented a house on the corner of Lafayette and Twenty-first streets, where they stayed two months, when they secured the house No. 1318 on Lafayette street, formerly the property of Councilman Aylesbury, paying $14 a month for it and giving the name of

THOMAS HOWARD.

The house is a one story cottage, painted white, with green shutters, and is romantically situated on the brow of a lofty eminence east of the city, commanding a fine view of the principal portion of the city, river and railroads, and adapted by nature for the perilous and desperate calling of Jesse James. Just east of the house is a deep, gulch-like ravine, and beyond that a broad expanse of open country backed by a belt of timber.

The house, except from the west side, can be seen for several miles. There is a large yard attached to the cottage, and a stable where Jesse had been keeping two horses, which were found there this morning.

Charles and Robert Ford have been occupying one of the rooms in the rear of the dwelling, and have secretly had an understanding to kill Jesse ever since last fall. A short time ago, before Robert had joined James, the latter proposed to rob the bank at Platte City. He said the

Burgess murder trial would commence there to-day and his plan was if they could get another companion to take a view of the situation and while the arguments were being heard in the murder case, which would naturally engage the attention of the citizens, boldly execute one of his

FAVORITE RAIDS.

Charley Ford approved of the plan, and suggested his brother Robert as a companion worthy of sharing the enterprise with them. Jesse had met the boy at the latter's house, near Richmond three years ago and consented to see him. The two men accordingly went to where Robert was, and arranged to have him accompany them to Platte City. As stated, all three came to St. Joe a week ago Sunday. They remained at the house all the week. Jesse thought it best that Robert should not exhibit himself on the premises, lest the presence of three able-bodied men who were doing nothing should excite suspicion.

They had fixed upon to-night to go to Platte City. Ever since the boys have been with Jesse they have watched for an opportunity to shoot him, but he was always so heavily armed that it was impossible to draw a weapon without James seeing it. They declare that they had no idea of taking him alive, considering the undertaking suicidal. The opportunity they had long wished for came this morning. Breakfast was over. Charley Ford and Jesse James had been in the stable currying the horses preparatory to their night ride. On returning to the room where Robert Ford was, Jesse said: "It's an awfully hot day." He pulled off his coat and vest and tossed them on the bed. Then he said, "I guess I'll take off my pistols for fear somebody will see them if I walk in the yard." He unbuckled the belt in which he carried two 45 caliber revolvers, one a Smith and Wesson and the other a Colt, and laid them on the bed with his coat and vest. He then picked up a dusting brush with the intention of dusting some pictures which hung on the wall. To do this he got on a chair. His back was now turned to the brothers, who silently stepped between

JESSE AND HIS REVOLVERS.

At a motion from Charley both drew their guns. Robert was the quickest of the two, and in one motion he had the long weapon to a level with his eye, with the muzzle not more than four feet from the back of the outlaw's head. Even in that motion, quick as thought, there was something which did not escape the acute ears of the hunted man. He made a motion as if to turn his head to ascertain the cause of that suspicious sound, but too late. A nervous pressure on the trigger, a quick flash, a sharp report and the well directed ball crashed through the outlaw's skull. There was no outcry; just a swaying of the body and it fell heavily backwards upon the carpet of the floor. The shot had been fatal and all the bullets in the chambers of Charley's revolver still directed at Jesse's head could not

MORE EFFECTUALLY

have decided the fate of the greatest bandit and free booter that ever figured in the pages of a country's history.

The ball had entered the base of the skull and made its way out through the forehead, over the left eye. It had been fired out of a Colt's 45 improved pattern, silver mounted and pearl handled pistol, presented by the dead man to his slayer only a few days ago.

Mrs. James was in the kitchen when the shooting was done, separated from the room in which the bloody tragedy occurred by the dining room. She heard the shot, and dropping her household duties ran into the front room. She saw her husband lying extended on his back, his slayers, each holding his revolver in his hand, making for the fence in the rear of the house. Robert had reached the inclosure, and was in the act of scaling it, when she stepped to the door, and calling to him: "Robert, you have done this, come back." Robert answered: "I swear to God I didn't." They then returned to where she stood. Mrs. James ran to the side of her husband and lifted his head. Life was not yet extinct, and when she asked him if he was hurt, it seemed to her that he wanted to say something, but could not. She tried

TO WASH AWAY

the blood that was coursing over his face from the hole in his forehead, but it seemed to her that the blood would come faster than she could wipe it away, and in her hands

JESSE JAMES DIED.

Charley Ford explained to Mrs. James that "a pistol had accidentally gone off." "Yes," said Mrs. James, "I guess it went off on purpose." Meanwhile Charley had gone back into the house and brought out two hats, and the two boys left the house. They went to the telegraph office, sent a message to Sheriff Timberlake, of Clay county; to Police Commissioner Craig, of Kansas City; to Gov. Crittenden, and other officers, and then surrendered themselves to Marshal Craig.

When the Ford boys appeared at the police station they were told by an officer that Marshal Craig and a posse of officers had gone in the direction of the James' residence, and they started after them and surrendered themselves. They accompanied the officers to the house and returned in custody of the police to the marshal's headquarters, where they were furnished with dinner and about 3 P.M. were removed to the old circuit court room where the inquest was held, in the presence of an immense crowd. Mrs. James

ACCOMPANIED THE OFFICERS

to the house having previously left her two children, ages 7 and 3 years, a boy and a girl, at the house of a Mrs. Turrel, who had known the Jameses under their assumed name of Howard ever since they had occupied the adjoining house. She was greatly affected by the tragedy, and the heart rending moans and expressions of grief were sorrowful evidence of the love she bore for the dead desperado.

The report of the killing of the notorious outlaw spread like wildfire through the city, and as usual the report assumed every variety of form and color. Very few accredited the news, however, and simply laughed at the idea that Jesse James was really the dead man.

Nevertheless, the excitement ran high, and when one confirming point succeeded the other, crowds of hundreds gathered at the undertaking establishment where lay the body. At the city hall, at the court house, and in fact on every street corner, the almost incredible news constituted the sole topic of conversation, to the exclusion of the barely less engrossing topic of the coming election.

HAROLD DELLINGER COLLECTION

Jesse's assassination, as portrayed in Outlaws of the Border (1882) *by Jay Donald.*

Coroner Heddins was notified, and undertaker Sidenfaden instructed to remove the body to his establishment. This was about 10 o'clock. A large crowd accompanied the coroner to the undertaker's, but only the wife and the reporters were admitted. The body lay in a remote room of the building. It had been taken out of the casket and placed upon a table. The features

APPEARED NATURAL,

but were disfigured by the bloody hole over the left eye. The body was neatly and cleanly dressed; in fact, nothing in the appearance of the remains indicated the desperate career of the man or the many bloody scenes of which he had been the hero. The large cavernous eyes were closed as in a calm slumber. Only the lower part of the face, the square cheek bones, the stout, prominent chin covered with a soft, sandy beard and the thin, firmly closed lips in a measure betrayed the determined will and iron courage of the dead man. A further inspection of the body revealed two large bullet wounds on the right side of the breast within three inches of the nipple, a bullet wound in the leg and the absence of the tip of the middle finger of the left hand.

After viewing the remains the coroner repaired to the court house, whither soon after Mrs. James, in custody of Marshal Craig, and the two Ford boys, both heavily armed, followed. They were kept in separate apartments until the jury announced itself ready

TO HEAR THE TESTIMONY.

The jury was empaneled as follows: W. H. Chouning, J. W. Moore, Warren Samuels, Thomas Norris, Wm. Turner, Wm. H. George. The witnesses examined were Mrs. James, the Ford boys, and James A. Little.

THE INQUEST BEGAN

with the examination of Mrs. James.

"What is your name?" Was the first question.

"Mrs. Jesse James."

"How long have you lived here?"

"I came here the 9th of last November."

"Where have you lived since then—at what place in this city?"

"We lived two months at Twenty-first and Lafayette streets. Since then in the house where my husband was killed."

"What kin was this man to you?"

"He was my husband."

"What was his name?"

"Jesse W. James."

"How long have you lived at this place where your husband was killed?"

"We moved there on Christmas eve."

"Who lived with you besides your husband?"

"Charlie Ford."

"Anybody else?"

"Nobody until last Sunday morning."

"Has he lived with you ever since you have been here?"

"Yes, sir."

"Has any one lived with you since last Sunday besides Charlie Ford?"

"Yes, sir."

"Who?"

"Robert Ford."

"What did this man live with you for?"

"They were afraid to stay at home, and my husband told them they could stay with us."

"Why were they afraid to stay at home?"

"There were charges against them, and they were afraid to stay at home."

"Where were you born?"

"In Kentucky."

"What is your age?"

"Thirty-five years."

"When were you married to Jesse James?"

"Eight years ago, the 24th of April."

"Whereabouts?"

"In Kearnay, Mo."

"Where have you lived since then?"

"Well, in different places. We have lived in Nashville, Tenn."

"Where else?"

"In Kansas City."

"When did you live in Kansas City?"

"Well, we left there on the 27th of last March."

"Well, now, Mrs. James, begin where you were married, and tell us where you first went, and where you have been up to this time."

"When we were first married we went to Texas."

"Did you go there first?"

"Yes, sir."

"How long did you live there?"

"About five months."

"Where did you go after that?"

"To Kansas City."

"How long did you live there?"

"Until the next November from the time I went there. It was about a year."

"What year was that?"

"I don't remember about what year. I cannot remember the date."

"Well, was it five or six years ago?"

"About six years I think?"

"Where did you live after that?"

"We went to Nashville, Tenn."

"How long did you live there?"

"Until last March."

"Where did you go then?"

"I went visiting some friends in Kentucky."

"Where was your husband then?"

"He was there part of the time."

"Has your husband been with you all this time since you were married?"

"Yes, sir, the greater part of the time."

"Where has he been at other times, can you tell?"

"Yes, I could tell, but I don't feel disposed to do so."

"Who was the party that married you?"

"Wm. James."

"Who was he?"

"A Methodist preacher."

"Where did he live?"

"In Kansas City."

"Were you married in Kansas City?"

"No, sir; in Kearney."

"Did he come from Kansas City to marry you?"

"Yes, sir."

"How many children have you?"

"Two."

"Are they both living?"

"Yes, sir."

"How long did you say you have been living here?"

"Since last November."

"What induced you to come here?"

"We came here to live as other people do."

"What occupation has your husband been in since you came here?"

"He has not been doing anything."

"How did he get a living?"

"He had a living without getting it."

"Have you had plenty all this time?"

"Yes, sir, and never suffered for anything."

"From whom did you rent this house?"

"Mrs. Thallton."

"Has he always been at home?"

"Yes, sir, except about two weeks, when he went to see his brother, and then went up into Nebraska."

"Who is his brother?"

"Johnson Samuels. He was wounded and was very low."

"Where was he wounded?"

"At Greenville at a party."

"Was he gone two weeks to see him?"

"No, sir, only one."

"Mrs. James, now please give us all the details of your husband's death."

"I was in the kitchen; my husband had gone from the room and had not been in there more than three minutes when I heard a pistol shot. I went right in, and he was lying on the floor. I looked at the door before I went into the room, and saw Rob. Johnson or Ford get over the fence. Charlie was standing in the yard. He came back. He said he did not do it; he would swear before God he didn't; that it was Bob. He was the one that shot him, I think, and then Charlie came in.

"Where was your husband when you went into this room?"

"I saw him lying on the floor"

"On his face?"

"No, sir, on his back."

"Was he dead when you went up to him?"

"No, sir; I could see signs of life."

"Did he breathe or speak?"

"I cannot tell whether he breathed or not. He did not speak."

"Had your husband always been friendly towards these boys, or had they had some trouble—fight or words?"

"No, sir; not a word that I ever knew of."

"Why were these boys living with your husband?"

"There were charges against them and they were afraid to stay at home."

"Do you know what any of the charges were?"

"They were charged with robbing a stage and being in a train robbery, and had been in the Blue Cut robbery; had robbed a stage between Lexington and some spring, I don't remember now what the name of it was."

"How do you know they were in these robberies?"

"I heard them say so. I heard Charlie say so."

"Which is the older of the two?"

"Charlie."

The inquest will be continued tomorrow.

ROBERT FORD.

Special Dispatch to the Kansas City Journal.

ST. JOSEPH, MO., April 3.—Bob Ford left Kansas City ten days ago for the purpose of capturing Jesse, dead or alive, and sent word to Commissioner Craig next day that he would have him here in ten days; would kill him if necessary on the first opportunity.

Bob is 21 years old, of boyish appearance, with smooth face; was raised in Clay county, and afterward the family removed to Ray county. The house of the Fords, in Ray county, was raided by the officers the first week in January, and it was this raid that resulted in the capture of Hite, and the killing of Jesse James.

Immediately after the visit of the officers negotiations were opened with the governor, Commissioner Craig and Sheriff Timberlake, for the surrender of Liddil.

Bob Ford came to Kansas City and had an interview with the governor at the St. James hotel on the night of the Craig Rifle ball. About three weeks after this Liddil surrendered to Timberlake and was brought to Kansas City with Bob Ford the same evening. Since then Liddil has been working faithfully with the officers for the capture of Jesse. The officers say he had given every evidence of good faith in the matter. Ford's house has been the rendezvous for the gang for two years. Jesse and Frank James were living in Nashville at the time of Ryan's capture, but shortly after his wife and family removed to Kansas City and commenced housekeeping a short distance east of the fair grounds, on Fourteenth street, one block east of Woodland avenue. The house is a small white frame of four rooms. Jesse and family lived there for three months. While in North Carolina Jesse was known as J. T. Jackson. In Nashville he was known as Howard, the same as in St. Joseph. On the 14th he removed to East Eighth street, just west of Woodland avenue near the Woodland school, on the north side of the street The house is a two-story frame. He lived there during the month of September and the first week in October, when they removed to St. Joe.

It was Jesse James who killed Conductor Westfall at the Winston train robbery. He also killed a farmer named Dan Askew. At the inquest Jesse James' wife said: "I came here November 9, lived two months on Twenty-first street; since then where my husband was killed. Charlie Ford lived with us. Last Sunday morning Robert came. These men were afraid to live at home. My husband told them they could stay with us.

"I was married to Jesse eight years ago the 24th of April, at Kearney. We went to Texas and staid about five months, then returned to Kansas City, where we lived about a year. We then went to Nashville, where we lived until last March. I could tell where my husband has been when not with me, but I am not disposed to do so. We were married by Wm. James, a Methodist preacher of Kansas City.

"Charlie and Robert were in the Blue Cut robbery and robbed a stage between Lexington and some springs."

In answer to the question, "Where is Frank James?" she said, "I know, but shan't tell." She said Jesse went to Nebraska recently to find a place to live where he could go to farming. She said he never went out without arms. He had two wounds in his breast and one in the leg. Henry H. Craig, Serg't Chas. Ditsch, Officer Nugent, Sheriff Timberlake and Dick Liddil came up to-night and tried to secure the release of the two Fords. They were unsuccessful in this, however. Gov. Crittenden will be here in the morning, and the men will undoubtedly be taken to Kansas City to-morrow.

Numberless wild rumors have been afloat about the attempt of friends of Jesse James to take the Fords from jail, and much uneasiness was felt there.

Dick Liddil asked to stay in jail, where he could be of assistance in case of trouble. Commissioner Craig, Sergeant Ditsch and Officer Nugent remained with the body of Jesse at the undertaker's through the night.

Charley Ford is a young man of genteel appearance, dressed in a neat grey coat and vest, black pants and stiff hat. He has black hair, large, cavernous brown eyes, and a prominent dimpled chin. Robert Ford has blonde hair, blue eyes, and is dressed in grey.

FROM

COLLECTED POEMS

By Max Douglas

1978

Coroner's Inquest Resumed

Wht is yr name?
Robert Ford.

How old are you?
Twenty years old.

—

Wht hv you bn doing in
Richmond?

Clerking in a grocery store.

Whn you left there where did you go?
I joind the detective force

& had a conversation wth Gov. Crittenden.

——

He told me wht he wd give
for the capture—sd he wd
give $10,000.00 a piece for
Jesse & Frank, dead or alive

——

He came over wth Ed Miller.
He & Jesse came to our house

one night in August.

Wht did they come for?
He was planning a robbery.

Was he introduced as anybody
else?

By the name of Jackson.
Did you know who he was?

How did you know?
Ed Miller told us so.

Did he know that you knew
who he was?

No, sir.

—

Where did they stay?

Stayd in the house during the
night & in the day time in
the corn fields & the timber.

—

Can you tell how you came
to kill him?

I had bn wth him every day
& night since last Sunday

week & this was the first
opportunity I hv had.

Hv you communicated wth
the governor yet?

I sent him a telegram as soon
as I shot him.

At this point a telegram from
Commissioner H. H. Craig of
Kansas City:

"*Will come on the first train.
Hurrah for you!*"

FROM

ADVENTURES OF A TRAMP PRINTER

By John Edward Hicks

1950

One night I was in the Buffalo saloon, near Fourth and Edmond. This place was originally so named because its first owner had come from Buffalo, New York. Shortly afterward, hunters killed an enormous buffalo on the site that later became Denver and brought the head across the plains as a trophy and for several decades it was the chief item of ornament in the saloon. Some of those present that night were along toward becoming high. One of them, a merchant, blurted out: "Boys, I've got seven hundred dollars on me, receipts from the store, and I'm afraid to start home with it; I've been hearing so much about highwaymen, especially about Jesse James." Someone suggested he spend the money right there in the Buffalo, thus obviating the necessity of going home and also the fear of bandits. One quiet gentleman in the crowd said: "My name is Tom Howard. I live out your way. I have two good pistols here and I know how to use them. If you want me to, I'll see that you get home unharmed." As the two were leaving, someone shouted,

JAMES FARM & MUSEUM, KEARNEY, MISSOURI

Robert Ford, the infamous assassin of Jesse James.

"What if you meet Jesse James?" Howard replied, "I'll never meet Jesse James. As for that, I'm as good a man as he is." It seemed to me I had seen Mr. Howard somewhere, but it was several days later before I remembered him as having been pointed out to me in the office of the Sedalia *Democrat.* He apparently proved a good guard, for the merchant reached home safely.

The morning of April 3, 1882, I had ambled up from the Galt House rather earlier than usual, anticipating something on account of the municipal election. Sam Wilson came hurrying toward me with "They've shot Jesse James! They've taken the body to Sidenfaden's! Come on, let's go see it!" I hurried along with Sam until we were milling about with the mass of people that thronged the undertaker's establishment. The crowd was not being admitted, but a reporter we knew being present to vouch for us, Sam and I were permitted to enter. Later they put Jesse in a coffin and propped him up in a window for all to see.

Sam and I walked out from the crowd, and inevitably toward the little house on Lafayette Street where Jesse under the name of Tom Howard had been living quietly with his wife and two children. It was a neat, well-painted cottage—still standing, by the way, but moved to another location as a show place. There were many Doubting Thomases in the street below the house, gazing at the place wherein the king of outlaws had lived—and died, particularly those who had seen the quiet-spoken, mild-mannered "Mr. Howard" going about the city, ostensibly interested in horses and occasionally making a trade. Some, to whom the name of Jesse James was a picaresque legend, said he never would have been killed in this fashion. He would have been slain in some bold dash of banditry. "Jesse James would never take off his pistols and turn his back on any living man," they would offer as a clincher and not without logic, for his apparent neglect which resulted in his immediate assassination remains to this day inexplicable.

FROM

BIOGRAPHY, MEMOIRS, REMINISCENCES AND RECOLLECTIONS

By John N. Edwards

1889

No one among all the hired cowards, hard on the hunt for blood money, dared face this wonderful outlaw, one even against twenty, until he had disarmed himself and turned his back to his assassins, the first and only time in a career which has passed from the realms of an almost fabulous romance into that of history.

We called him outlaw, and he was, but Fate made him so. When the war came he was just turned of fifteen. The border was all aflame with steel, and fire, and ambuscade, and slaughter. He flung himself into a band which had a black flag for a banner and devils for riders. What he did he did, and it was fearful. But it was war. It was Missouri against Kansas. It was Jim Lane and Jennison against Quantrell, Anderson and Todd.

When the war closed Jesse James had no home. Proscribed, hunted, shot, driven away from among his people, a price put upon his head—what else could the man do, with such a nature, except what he did do? He had to live. It was his country. The graves of his kindred were there. He refused to be banished from his birthright, and when he was hunted he turned savagely about and hunted his hunters. Would to God he were alive to-day to make a righteous butchery of a few more of them.

There never was a more cowardly and unnecessary murder committed in all America than this murder of Jesse James. It was done for money. It was done that a few might get all the money. He had been living in St. Joseph for months. The Fords were with him. He was in the toils, for they meant to betray him. He was in the heart of a large city. One word would have summoned 500 armed men for his capture or extermination. Not a single one of the attacking party need to have been hurt. If, when his house had been surrounded, he had refused to surrender, he could have been killed on the inside of it and at long range. The chances for him to escape were as one to 10,000, and not even that; but it was never intended that he should be captured. It was his blood the bloody wretches were after—blood that would bring money in the official market of Missouri.

And this great commonwealth leagued with a lot of self confessed robbers, highwaymen and prostitutes to have one of its citizens assassinated, before it was positively known he had ever committed a single crime worthy of death.

Of course everything that can be said about the dead man to justify the manner of his killing, will be said; but who is saying it? Those with the blood of Jesse James on their guilty souls. Those who conspired to murder him. Those who wanted the reward and would invent any lie or concoct any diabolical story to get it. They have succeeded, but such a cry of horror and indignation at the infernal deed is even now thundering over the land that if a single one of the miserable assassins had either manhood, conscience, or courage, he would go, as another Judas, and hang himself. But so sure as God reigns, there never was a dollar of blood-money obtained yet which did not bring with it perdition. Sooner or later there comes a day of vengeance. Some among the murderers are mere beasts of prey. These, of course, can only suffer through cold, or hunger or thirst; but whatever they dread most that thing will happen. Others again among the murderers are sanctimonious devils who plead the honor of the State, the value of law and order, the splendid courage required to shoot an unarmed man in the back of the head; and these will be stripped to their skin of all their pretensions, and made to shiver and freeze, splotched as they are and spotted and piebald with blood, in the pitiless storm of public contempt and condemnation. This to the leaders will be worse than death.

Nor is the end yet. If Jesse James had been hunted down as any other criminal, and killed while trying to escape or in resisting arrest, not a word would have been said to the contrary. He had sined and he had suffered. In his death the majesty of the law would have been vindicated; but here the law itself becomes a murderer. It leagues with murderers. It hires murderers. It aids and abets murderers. It borrows money to pay and reward murderers. It promises immunity and protection to murderers. It is itself a murderer—the most abject, the most infamous, and the most cowardly ever known to history. Therefore this so-called law is an outlaw, and these so-called executors of the law are outlaws. Therefore let Jesse James' comrades—and he has a few remaining worth all the Fords and Littles that could be packed together between St. Louis and St. Joe—do unto them as they did unto him. Yes, the end is not yet, nor should it be. The man had no trial. What right had any officer of this State to put a price upon his head and hire a band of cut-throats and highwaymen to murder him for money?

Anything can be told of man. The whole land is filled with liars and robbers, and assassins. Murder is easy for a hundred dollars. Nothing is safe that is pure or unsuspecting, or just, but it is not to be supposed that the law will become an ally and a co-worker in this sort of a civilization. Jesse James has been murdered, first, because an immense price had been set upon his head, and there isn't a low-lived scoundrel to-day in Missouri who wouldn't kill his own father for money; and second, because he was made the scape-goat of every train-robber, foot-pad and highwayman between Iowa and Texas. Worse men a thousand times than the dead man have been hired to do this thing. The very character of the instruments chosen shows the infamous nature of the work required. The hand that slew him had to be a traitor's! Into all the warp and woof of the devil's work there were threads woven by the fingers of a harlot. What a spectacle! Missouri, with splendid companies and regiments of militia. Missouri, with a hundred and seventeen sheriffs, as brave and as efficient on the average as any men on earth. Missouri, with a watchful and vigilant marshal in every one of her principal towns and cities. Missouri, with every screw and cog and crank and lever and wheel of her administrative machinery in perfect working order. Missouri, with all her order, progress and development, had yet to surrender all these in the face of a single man—a hunted, lied-upon, proscribed and outlawed man, trapped and located in the midst of thirty-five thousand people—and ally with some five or six cut-throats and prostitutes that the majesty of the law might be vindicated, and the good name of the State saved from all further reproach! Saved! Why, the whole State reeks to-day with a double orgy—that of lust and that of murder. What the men failed to do, the women accomplished.

Tear the two bears from the flag of Missouri. Put thereon, in place of them, as more appropriate, a thief blowing out the brains of an unarmed victim, and a brazen harlot, naked to the waist and splashed to the brows in blood.

FROM

COLLECTED POEMS

By Max Douglas

1978

The Personal Property Of

Received of E. Craig, per Jos.
Finley, the following articles, viz.

1 set (3) pearl & jet shirt studs
1 gold collar button
1 heavy gold ring markd "Jesse"
1 pair jet & gold ear pendants
1 jet & gold breast pin
1 pair gold & jet sleeve buttons

1 book entitled "Noted Guerrillas" by
Edwards

3 half cases ambrotype pictures
2 small double case ambrotypes

(2 in 1)
1 small open case ambrotype
1 leather bound ambrotype containing
1 picture
2 double case ambrotypes containing
1 picture (each)
1 small round case containing
1 picture
1 photograph album & ambrotypes
containing 15 pictures

—

One breech loading shot gun,
one Winchester rifle,
one Smith & Wesson revolver,
two scabbards,
one bundle of wearing apparel,
one saddle & bridle; one saddle.

MESSAGE OF GOV. THOMAS T. CRITTENDEN TO THE THIRTY-SECOND GENERAL ASSEMBLY OF THE STATE OF MISSOURI

1883

OUTLAWRY

Since the close of the war Missouri has been infested by bands of train and bank robbers, whose lawless deeds not only rendered railroad travel and banking dangerous, in certain localities in the State, but also gave the State an unenviable reputation, at home and abroad.

My predecessors assiduously endeavored, by the use of every means and power within their control, to accomplish the destruction of these bands, but their efforts proved abortive. On the 15th day of July, 1881, certain parties, under the leadership of Jesse W. James, stopped and robbed a train upon the line of the Chicago, Rock Island and Pacific Railroad, at a point near Winston, in Daviess county; and, in the perpetration of the robbery, killed William Westfall, the conductor of the train, and John McCulloch, an employee of the company. On the 28th day of July, 1881, I issued the following proclamation:

STATE OF MISSOURI, EXECUTIVE DEPARTMENT.

"WHEREAS, It has been made known to me, as the Governor of the State of Missouri, that certain parties, whose names are to me unknown, have confederated and banded themselves together for the purpose of committing robberies and other depredations within this State; and

"WHEREAS, Said parties did, on or about the eighth day of October, 1879, stop a train near Glendale, in the county of Jackson, in said State, and with force and violence, take, steal and carry away the money and other express matter being carried thereon; and

"WHEREAS, On the 15th day of July, 1881, said parties and their confederates did stop a train upon the line of the Chicago, Rock Island and Pacific Railroad, near Winston, in the county of Daviess, in said State, and with force and violence, take, steal and carry away the money and other express matter being carried thereon, and in perpetration of the robbery last aforesaid the parties engaged therein, did kill and murder one William Westfall, the conductor of the train, together with one John McCulloch, who was at the time in the employ of said company then on said train; and

"WHEREAS, Frank James and Jesse W. James stand indicted in the circuit court of said Daviess county, for the murder of John W. Sheets, and the parties engaged in the robberies and murders aforesaid have fled from justice and have absconded and secreted themselves;

Now, therefore, in consideration of the premises, and in lieu of all other rewards heretofore offered for the arrest or conviction of the parties aforesaid, or either of them, by any person or corporation, I, Thomas T. Crittenden, Governor of the State of Missouri, do hereby offer a reward of Five Thousand Dollars ($5,000.00) for the arrest and conviction of each person participating in either of the robberies or murders aforesaid, excepting the said Frank James and Jesse W. James; and for the arrest and delivery of said Frank James and Jesse W. James, and each or either of them to the sheriff of said Daviess county, I hereby offer a reward of Five Thousand Dollars ($5,000.00), and for the conviction of either of the parties last aforesaid of participation in either of the murders or robberies above mentioned, I hereby offer a further reward of Five Thousand Dollars ($5,000.00).

IN TESTIMONY WHEREOF, I have hereunto set my hand and caused to be affixed the great seal of the State of Missouri. Done at the City of Jefferson on this 28th day of July, A. D. 1881.

By the Governor:
THOS T. CRITTENDEN.
MICH'L K. MCGRATH,
Secretary of State.

On the 7th day of September, 1881, within six weeks after this proclamation had been issued, as if in grim defiance of the power of the law and the vigilance of law officers, a train was stopped and robbed on the line of the Chicago and Alton Railroad, near Blue Cut, in Jackson county. The band committing this robbery was under the leadership of Jesse W. James; and his associates, it is said, were Frank James, Dick Liddil, Wood Hite, Clarence Hite and Charles and Robert Ford.

When the proclamation was issued, it was said by cavillers that it would wholly fail in its objects and that no good would be accomplished by the offer of such large sums of money for the apprehension of those desperate men. The results which followed so closely upon its issuance furnish an ample vindication of the policy which inspired it. No tie, no faith in honorable comradeship, is stronger with an outlaw than the power of money.

On the 13th day of February, 1882, Bob Ford surrendered to Capt H. H. Craig of Kansas City. On the 24th day of January, 1882, Dick Liddil surrendered to J. R. Timberlake, sheriff of Clay county.

On the 13th day of February, 1882, Clarence Hite was captured in Logan county, Kentucky, by Capt. Craig and J. R. Timberlake, and was taken to Daviess county, Missouri, where two indictments—one for the murder of William Westfall and one for participation in the Winston train robbery—were pending against him. He was arraigned under the indictment and pleaded guilty to the charge of robbery, and was, on the same

LIBRARY OF CONGRESS, LC-DIG-CWPBH-04801

Thomas T. Crittenden, Governor of Missouri and architect of a plan to end outlawry in Missouri.

day, sentenced to twenty-five years imprisonment in the penitentiary, which sentence he is now undergoing.

On the 3d day of April, 1882, Jesse W. James was killed in the city of St. Joseph by Charles and Robert Ford—his followers and associates in crime. The Fords immediately surrendered themselves to the legal authorities of Buchanan county and were placed in jail.

An indictment charging them with murder in the first degree, was preferred against them by a grand jury, to which, at the April term, 1882, they both pleaded guilty in the Buchanan county circuit court, and were pardoned by me on the same day, upon grounds of public policy.

Frank James voluntarily surrendered himself to me, in my office, in Jefferson City, on the 5th day of October, 1882. I immediately delivered him to the law officers of Jackson county, where he is now incarcerated in jail, awaiting trial on one or more indictments.

On the 4th day of December, 1881, Wood Hite was killed by some one of his confederates in crime, at the residence of Mrs. Bolton, near Richmond, Ray county, Missouri. Her house had been the headquarters and hiding place of the outlaws, in that part of the State, for many months.

On the 13th day of May, 1882, Robert Ford was indicted in Ray county for the murder of Wood Hite. The case was removed, by change of venue, to Clinton county where, on the 26th day of October, 1882, he was tried and acquitted. He is now under recognizance on a charge of robbery, as also is his brother, Charles Ford.

On the 7th day of October, 1882, I revoked the proclamation of July 28th, 1881, for the reason that the principal actors in, and perpetrators of, the crimes are either dead or are in the custody of the laws of the State.

Thus was completed the overthrow and destruction of the most noted and daring band of outlaws known to ancient or modern history. This grand result, fraught with so much interest and importance to the people of Missouri, was accomplished by the activity and relentless energy of the officers and citizens of this State, and particularly of those in the localities in which the outlaws had so long found sympathy and concealment. The policy adopted for the extirpation of these bands received the co-operation of the Criminal Court of Jackson county and its officers; and thus there was but little difficulty in securing a pronounced enforcement of the laws, and awakening in the minds of the people of that county a settled determination to remove the stain placed upon the county by the depredations of these bands, and to summarily end, at once, and forever, the crimes and career of the organization. In this connection, I desire to publicly recognize the intelligent and efficient assistance of Capt. Henry H. Craig of Kansas City, and Sheriff James R. Timberlake of Clay county. The aid rendered by these gentlemen was invaluable to me, and without it the duty devolving upon me would have been much more difficult, if not altogether impossible, to accomplish. The task they assumed required fearless courage, extraordinary vigilance and an unerring selection of instrumentalities. They accomplished within fourteen months what others for twenty years had wholly failed to do; and to these gentlemen, more than to all others, is due the credit of bringing these outlaws to justice. It also gives me pleasure to recognize the valuable services of John Cason, sheriff of Saline county, who was always ready to undergo any labor, danger or exposure in pursuit of the outlaws. In him Captains Craig and Timberlake had an intelligent and faithful coadjutor. These brave officers discharged every duty fearlessly and well, to which I unhesitatingly bear official testimony.

I paid twenty thousand dollars in rewards to various persons for the capture and overthrow of this band of desperadoes, not one dollar of which was taken from the State Treasury. It is not probable that Missouri will again be cursed and disgraced by the presence of such a band of men, confederated together for desperate purposes. It is fully redeemed and acquit of that unwarranted appellation of "robber State." But an insignificant number of people in two or three counties gave countenance to such lawlessness. Our people, with one accord, heartily approve of the measures and means employed to compel these violators of the law to confess its power and majesty, and applaud the stern, unbending determination of the officers who contributed so much to the fulfillment of that purpose.

It is done; and Missouri is to-day one of the most peaceful States in the Union. Fewer crimes are committed within her borders than in those of surrounding States.

FROM

SINGING RAWHIDE: A BOOK OF WESTERN BALLADS

By Harold Hersey

1926

The Death of Jesse James

Jesse wuz a bandit, yeh! and a two-gun guy;
He'd hold up a train with a twinkle in hiz eye,
And hiz best pard killed him, like a coward on thuh sly.

Take up yore dallies,
Rope yore mavericks,
It's a damn pore cowboy
What don't know hiz tricks.

Jesse warn't no cowboy, but he knew thuh old frontiers;
He'd rob a money-lender and he'd soothe a widder's tears,

And he's got 'er reppertation that'll last a million years.

Gather 'round the campfire,
Mend your hackamore,
I likes ter talk on Jesse
And the old Civil War.

Jesse and hiz brother Frank wuz guerrillas to thuh bone,
When thuh War wuz over they tried tuh carry it on alone,
And they purty near succeeded if thuh truth wuz only known.

I'm an ancient top-hand now,
I wuz only a youngster then,
But I'm here ter tell thuh world
In them days, men wuz men.

At Paso Robel Jesse James met hiz brother Frank
Restin' after makin' a raid on thuh Russellville bank. . .
Jesse, handsome Jesse James; hiz brother lean and lank.

They'd lost old Ollie Shepherd,
One o' Quantrell's trusty souls,
Who'd died rather'n surrender,
Full o' bullet holes.

In California Jesse lived thuh narrow and thuh straight,

But he had a lot 'er enemies who followed him with
hate,
And when he'd robbed the Gallatin, Lor', it wuz too
late.

I don't like idle prattle,
Advice ain't in my line,
But I thank thuh stars above me
Bob Ford's soul ain't mine.

Ford followed Jesse James to thuh place where he
wuz hid,
Like Judas sellin' out hiz God he wuz bought for
thuh highest bid;
And he shot him in thuh back, leavin' a widder and
a kid.

Up there in thuh starry heaven
Before thuh mighty Lord
I'd rather be in Jesse's shoes
Than in those of Robert Ford.

FROM

THE RISE AND FALL OF JESSE JAMES

By Robertus Love

1940

Jesse James had two burials but only one funeral. I witnessed the second burial, which took place twenty years after the first. On that occasion I made up my mind to tell the world, so far as might lie within my ability, the truth about Jesse James. This narrative, written more than twenty-three years later, is the outcome of that purpose.

Although familiar for many years with the birthplace and the two burial places of the most widely known of the Missouri outlaws, it was not until a pleasant afternoon in the March of 1925 that I visited the house where he was killed. It no longer is "the little white house with the green shutters." The white paint has been supplanted by a coat of fading brown. The shutters have disappeared. The stable in the rear, where the distinguished tenant kept his two horses ready for fast flight, also has disappeared. The street in front has been cut down about eight feet to grade, leaving a ragged bank a rod from the house. Tacked on the outer wall just to the right of the front door—through which the Fords ran out after the assassination—I found a small board bearing the words "Jessie James House—Admission 15 Cents."

When Mrs. Mary Dycus, widow of Francis Marion Dycus and for twenty-one years tenant of the historic cottage, admitted me to the front chamber in which the outlaw was slain, I handed her thirty cents, and she looked behind me for the other visitor. I was alone. Mrs. Dycus was grateful. I called her attention to the feminine misspelling of Jesse's Christian name on the placard. The widow smiled.

"That's the Missouri of it," she explained; "I didn't make that sign myself."

Mrs. Dycus is not a native. Since her husband with the Revolutionary fighter's name died a few years ago she has lived alone in the house of the tragedy.

"Don't you get a bit scary here?" I inquired.

"Scary—what at?"

"Why, at—well, at Jesse James' ghost, for instance."

"Huh! the only ghosts I ever see are live ones. And I wouldn't be scared of Jesse James if he came back here, anyhow. He'd never harm a woman, I'm certain. There's lots of worse men than he was. These bandits we've got today are a whole lot worse; they are so awful mean and cruel."

"Mrs. Dycus," I said, "I fully agree with you; the facts prove you perfectly correct."

In my coat pocket I carried a copy of the St. Joseph *News-Press* of that very day. On the front page was a dispatch from New York City under these headlines: "BEATEN BY BANDITS, ROBBED OF $50,000—Three Masked Men Chop Way into New York Woman's Apartment—Bite Rings from Fingers—Mrs. Fay Perkins Tortured Until She Reveals Jewelry—Burglars Believed Gangsters That Murdered Two Victims."

Mrs. Dycus has a picture on the wall at the spot where hung the one that Jesse James was dusting when he was shot. She said that the one Jesse was dusting was a likeness of "Skyrocket," his favorite horse. Jesse dearly loved horses. The Ford boys said shortly after they killed him that he was "the most expert horse thief in the Middle West," but they added that he never took horses for gain but merely for use in emergencies, and that he always returned them or paid for them later when he could do so without peril. This I know, from more reliable evidence, to have been a fact. An outlaw of strange parts, that Jesse James!

Mrs. Dycus said that many persons visit the old house, women seeming to be particularly curious about the bandit. She showed me through the four rooms of the cottage. There was a kitchen at the rear, in the Jesse James days; it has disappeared, and the James dining room is the Dycus kitchen. The house belongs now to the city, having been taken over because of unpaid taxes.

"It's nice and quiet up here on this hill," remarked Mrs. Dycus; "I like it here—right nice place to live at."

Jesse James liked it. He could see about him in all directions and take note of any suspicious-looking person approaching. But he liked life on a farm still better: it was safer, for one thing. There is good reason for the belief that in his last days he was hoping he might be able to buy a farm in Nebraska and settle down to make a living by agriculture. The Fords said he had not "done any job" since the Blue Cut train robbery of the preceding September. He was laying plans, they declared, to rob a bank at Platte City, Missouri, and they had agreed to assist. He had only about $700 or $800 on hand. Three weeks before his death he had visited Pawnee, Nebraska, registering at the local hotel as Tom Howard of St. Joseph. He wished to rent a house there, he stated, and he looked at outlying farms with a view to purchase.

In the days following the assassination, St. Joseph was rife with stories of rich local color anent the slain bandit. Mr. Howard, the preceding winter, had entertained the Ferrell girls at 1320 Lafayette Street, adjoining his home, by playing with them at snowballing. He was an expert marksman with a snowball, and when one of the girls hit him with a snowy missile he took it with great good nature. "He laughed like a schoolboy," the girls recalled.

Mr. Howard was a regular customer of August Brokaw, a druggist on lower Sixth Street. He became a warm favorite there. He bought cigars to give to his friends—including the Fords. Nearly every day he would sit in the drug store and tell stories—clean ones, stories with points. He told Brokaw he was a railroad man out of a job. The druggist promised to get him a railroad job! Undoubtedly Mr. Howard laughed, upsleeve, at this. After all, and after a fashion, Jesse enjoyed life. Major Edwards wrote, comparing the two brothers: "Jesse laughed at many things, Frank laughed not at all. Jesse was lighthearted, reckless, devil-may-care; Frank was sober, sedate, a splendid man always for ambush or scouting parties. Both were undaunted."

Mr. Howard liked to play billiards. Late one night, after a game in a St. Joseph billiard hall, another player remarked to him that he was afraid to go home alone—he might be held up and robbed. Mr. Howard volunteered to escort the fearsome citizen home. At the man's door he called out a cheery good night.

Under caption of "Worthy of Notice," the *Gazette* said on April 6, 1882: "It is positively known that Jesse James attended the Sunday services at the Presbyterian church, opposite the World's Hotel, repeatedly. Last Sunday he was seen with his entire family at the Union Depot, viewing the improvements."

The same newspaper stated that rain fell ceaselessly as Mrs. Jesse James and Mrs. Zerelda Samuel were removing the effects from the house, after the inquest. Some of the effects had been removed by the officials. These included a shotgun, two revolvers, two watches, two watch-chains, a diamond ring, a gold ring, a breastpin, shirt buttons, a pair of cuff buttons with coral setting, a pin with the initials "J. W. J." on it—and one of Mrs. James' earrings. The property was returned to the family.

Another article observed in the house was a well-worn Bible. Mrs. James, when asked by a newspaper reporter if her husband ever read it, replied:

"Yes, he read it very often."

Now, by this roundabout route, we approach the funeral and first burial of Jesse James. A St. Joseph dispatch of April 5 to the Kansas City *Times* said:

> "Craig and Timberlake, the principal men who engineered Jesse's capture [*sic*], have been delayed and obstructed all day by the St. Joseph officials, through jealousy. The special train has been waiting since 10 A.M. to take the body, but the city marshal would not give it up. The body was not secured until 6 P.M. and taken quietly to the depot, where Sheriff Timberlake's party prepared to go out on the regular train to Cameron. From there they go by a special to Kearney. Jesse's widow, children and mother accompany the remains. They are very nervous. The body is in a $500 coffin furnished by Craig and Timberlake. The funeral will take place tomorrow."

The *Times* correspondent wrote that "a perfect mob was at the depot to see the party off." Mrs. Samuel insisted that she be taken to the baggage car to see the body put on the train. Timberlake and his party sat in the baggage car as guards.

> "Mrs. James was accompanied by Luther James, a cousin of Jesse's, from Kansas City. While in the depot at St. Joseph a short, thickset man tried to pull a pistol on Mrs. Samuel but was promptly thrown out of the door and landed in the street. He was shot at, but not hit.
>
> "At all stations along the road crowds gathered, anxious to see the body, the family, the officers, or anything, and great excitement prevailed. We arrived at Cameron at 9.11 P.M. and were met by an immense crowd. The ladies were taken to a private room at the depot while waiting for the train, and the body was taken from the baggage car, followed by a mob who stood around the windows, eager to catch a glimpse of the pine box that enveloped the coffin. Mrs. Samuel and Mrs. James are very much worn out.

A dispatch received here by Mrs. Samuel says her youngest son is dying at home."

There was delay in getting the special train, but at last the special came, and the party departed at midnight for Kearney. The train was furnished by officials of the Rock Island railroad. It will be remembered that it was a train of the Rock Island system that suffered in the first train robbery, nearly nine years earlier. It is surmisable that the officials of that line were glad to extend this final courtesy.

The train reached Kearney at 2.45 A.M. The baggage car that carried the corpse was sidetracked. The rest of the rolling stock pulled out to continue traffic on the esteemed Rock Island. Mrs. Samuel, wearied and worried, hastened out to the farmhouse to reach the bedside of John T. Samuel, her son, a youth of twenty who had been shot in a scrimmage at a neighborhood "party" a few nights earlier. He was believed to be dying, but he recovered. At this writing Mr. Samuel is living at Long Beach, Calif.

The casket was placed upon two chairs in the office of the Kearney House, the small local hotel. After daylight the lid was removed. Throughout the forenoon the body of Jesse James "lay in state" in his old home town. Many persons passed by to view the dead face and folded hands. Old acquaintances said the corpse "looked natural." Hundreds of oldtime residents saw Jesse for the first time. Some Kearneyites said they had seen him before but had been unaware of his interesting identity.

Funeral services were held in the afternoon at the Kearney Baptist church of which Jesse had been a member. The pallbearers were five local men and a mysterious stranger. Nobody seemed to know this man, who appeared to be somewhat in authority.

"It's Frank James!" whispered a spectator, hoarsely.

But it was a stout man, and Frank James was slender. Two clergymen took part in the services, which opened with the singing of "What a Friend We Have in Jesus," a hymn sung frequently by Jesse in boyhood and when he was a church member—and probably after he was "excluded." The Rev. R. H. Jones of Lathrop, Missouri, read the passage from the book of Job beginning "Man that is born of woman is of few days and full of trouble." He read also two verses from the Thirty-ninth Psalm, beginning "Lord, make me to know mine end."

After a fervent prayer by the Rev. Mr. Jones, the funeral sermon was preached by the Rev. J. M. P. Martin, pastor of the church. His text was Matthew 24:44, "Therefore be ye ready, for in such an hour as ye think not the Son of Man cometh." He said, by way of introduction, "It would be useless for me to bring any new information before this congregation respecting the life and character of the deceased." That was his sole allusion to the dead man. The sermon was an appeal to all present to bear in mind the transitory nature of the earthly pilgrimage and to be ready for the ultimate and inevitable transition.

In closing, Pastor Martin stated that Mrs. Samuel wished him to request that those present refrain from going out to the farm, where interment was to take place. John Samuel, he said, was lying very low, and as the grave was quite near the house it was feared that the gathering of a crowd might affect the patient seriously. "It is therefore requested that none but friends and relatives go to the grave."

When the cortège reached the Samuel farmhouse a considerable number of country folk had gathered there. All were quiet and respectful, as befitted the solemn occasion. Jesse James was buried in a corner of the yard, on the premises where he was born, where his mother could look from her windows upon the mound at the foot of a big coffee-bean tree. Mrs. Samuel planted flowers upon the grave, and for twenty years she tended them with affectionate care. A tall white marble monument was erected there, on which the mother had this inscription carved:

In Loving Remembrance of My Beloved Son
JESSE W. JAMES
Died April 3, 1882
Aged 34 years, 6 Months, 28 Days
Murdered by a Traitor and Coward Whose
Name is Not Worthy to Appear Here

And so at last the world's most hunted man—and according to his friends the most hounded—after nearly twenty years of warring and worrying, came home to rest undisturbed for another score of years.

"JESSE JAMES AS ROBIN HOOD"

By Sam Sackett

1980

None of the good badmen with which American legendry is well supplied is better known than Jesse James, whose story has persisted for nearly a century in the memories of his compatriots. Although we must recognize at the outset that we are in an area where certitude is impossible, it is interesting to speculate about the reasons why Jesse has become a household word. Such speculation was anticipated by Mody Boatright in the last paragraph of his article on "The Western Bad Man as Hero"; with so reputable a jurist having signed our warrant, let us proceed. I contend there are reasons intrinsic to the outlaw's profession why any practitioner thereof might be considered a hero and, moreover, reasons why that was especially true at the time during which Jesse and his band operated. But these reasons still do not explain why he, rather than some other outlaw, captured the folk imagination. Those reasons lie in the fact that, as Kent Steckmesser has already demonstrated, most of Jesse's story is composed of common legend motifs.

Let us begin with the causes intrinsic to Jesse's chosen profession. Jesse was known as the American Robin Hood; as the song says, "He robbed from the rich, and he gave to the poor." The identification of Jesse with Robin Hood brings to mind Steckmesser's observation that other popular outlaws share the reputation of being, in some kind of individualistic, non-institutional way, agents of social reform and the redistribution of the wealth. Evidently there is something about outlawry that causes the contemporary popular mind to view its practitioners in this way.

"He robbed from the rich." Let us meditate on this a moment from the standpoint of a young man who is standing on the threshold of a career in banditry, seeking to determine the principles which will allow him to succeed in his chosen line of work. "He robbed from the rich." Who else? What sense would it make to rob from the poor? Each strike, after all, may be viewed by a bandit as a kind of investment, into which he puts a certain amount of planning, a certain amount of effort, and a certain amount of risk. Like any other investor, he seeks the highest return on his outlay. I believe it was Willie Sutton who once told a questioner the reason he robbed all those banks: "That was where the money was."

"And he gave to the poor." Let us meditate also on this concept for a moment. You have just robbed a bank and gotten a lot of money. What are you going to do with it? Put it in a savings account? That's where it just came from! You know, better than anyone else, how prone banks are to lose their depositors' money. No, the only sensible thing to do with the results of a robbery is to spend it. That's what money's for, isn't it? And if you don't spend it quick, the sheriff may get you before you get all the good out of it. Then, when it's gone, you can always get more. "Shine, Mister?" "Sure, Kid. Here's a five-dollar gold piece, and keep the change." "What'll it be for you, Gents?" "Drinks for everybody on me. And say, Barkeep, here's a double eagle for your trouble." It is probably significant in this relation to notice a couplet from the ballad of Sam Bass: "He fairly coined the money, and he spent it rather free, / And he always drank good whiskey wherever he might be." These are likely the ways in which Jesse James also became know as a Robin Hood by the poor people with whom he came into contact. They may help explain why so many people were reluctant to turn him in. And they make us curious about how the original Robin Hood became known as a Robin Hood.

In addition to the reasons which lie in the circumstances of outlawry themselves, we may find some in the historical period in which Jesse operated—the post–Civil War milieu, the activities of banks in hard times, and the expansion of the railroads. Mody Boatright, indeed, has linked all three of these by pointing out that the railroads, express companies, and banks were "instruments of Yankee exploitation," and the same is implied by Marshall W. Fishwick; Boatright also links the growth of the James legend to populism.

To begin with, we should take note of Jesse's Southern affiliations, which were significant in a career which really got under way in 1866. Frank James, of course, had ridden with Quantrill's band of irregular Confederate raiders; Jesse himself may have done so as well. It was not only the local constabularies who were after the James gang: it was also, on a number of occasions, the Federal troops. His hard-to-catchness must have seemed droll and dear to many a Confederate veteran made to feel something of an outlaw himself under the punitive Reconstruction legislation sponsored by the so-called radical Republicans. From a tactical standpoint, too, the techniques of the James gang are related to the strike-and-run military methods adapted by several Confederate leaders—Quantrill himself, of course, but also John Singleton Mosby, the Gray Ghost. More significantly, there were actions in which Stonewall Jackson and Jeb Stuart likewise made good use of, first, a rapid cavalry attack which surprised the enemy and, then, an equally rapid retreat which baffled pursuit. The similarity in tactics could hardly have gone unnoticed by former Johnny Rebs, who may well have viewed the James boys as somehow paying Them back for Appomattox.

More importantly, however, the period just after the Civil War was marked by much land speculation and similar economic development which boomed into the Panic of 1873. Jesse and his friends began their activities in 1866, the year which is referred to in American economic history as the beginning of the postwar depression. As the subsequent boom began to develop, the American farmer—as usual—did not get a fair share of the prosperity; when the Panic of 1873 hurt everyone, it hurt farmers worst of all; and farm income did not really begin to rise again until 1879, when there was a serious crop failure in Europe. During the period 1866–1879, which coincides with the greatest activity of the James gang, a great many farmers, not only in Missouri but throughout the United States, found it impossible to repay their bank loans and lost their land on mortgage foreclosures; the popular fiction and drama of the period are full of such incidents. Here it is important to remember that Jesse James is important in the history of American crime because if he did not invent the bank holdup, he developed it and brought it to a high art. He is the Sophocles of American bank robbers. It would be hard for an ex-farmer, thrown off his land by foreclosure, not to feel that Jesse was retaliating against his oppressor.

George D. Hendricks has also related the James legend to antagonism toward the railroads. The period of James's greatest activity was also a period of enormous expansion by the railroads, as they tried to make up for the war-enforced inactivity of the previous four years. We may recall that 1867 was the year of the Credit Mobilier scandal; two years later Jay Cooke was appointed financial agent for the Northern Pacific, and the Central Pacific and Union Pacific met at Promontory Point.

These facts give us a mental image of twin ribbons of steel being laid across open prairie, viewed only by hostile Indians and puzzled buffalo. But there was railroad building in more populous areas, such as Missouri, as well. According to Henry V. Poor's *Manual of the Railroads of the United States for 1876–77*, between 1860 and 1866 only 108 miles of railroad were built in Missouri; whereas in 1867, 160 miles were built, in 1868, 269 miles, in 1869, 358 miles, and so on. Between 1866 and 1870 the number of miles of railroad track in Missouri more than doubled, reaching two thousand miles in the latter year, and an additional thousand miles of track had been laid by 1876. In the year 1871 alone, 580 miles of track were built. Some of these railroads, of course, were built on unused land which the roads had obtained from the federal government; the St. Louis, Iron Mountain, and Southern, for instance, had obtained land grants from the government in 1852–53, although it did not lay track on them until the years between 1867 and 1872. But many railroads were moving across land which was more settled, and there were land-condemnation proceedings in which farmers had their land taken away from them; doubtless they felt that the judges and juries were in the pay of the railroads and that the compensation awarded them for their farms was pitifully inadequate. Thus while townsmen encouraged the building of railroads, farmers were generally less than enthusiastic.

It will be recalled that the James boys came from northwest Missouri, having been born in the county where North Kansas City is now located, not far from much railroad activity. The Kansas City, St. Joseph, and Council Bluffs Rail Road began laying track in 1866 and was completed in 1874; the Hannibal and St. Joseph Railway, which had been built in 1859 with 207 miles of track, added 68 miles to its road in 1867; the St. Joseph and St. Louis Railroad was completed in 1870; the St. Joseph, Kansas, and Texas Railway began selling bonds for a projected road in 1873 and bought fifty miles of right-of-way as a prelude to commencing operations the same year. It may not be entirely coincidence that that was also the year in which Jesse James, who had already proved himself a great technical innovator by his development of the bank robbery, first applied himself, with similar originality and flair, to robbing trains.

Another cause for hostility between the railroad and the farmer is suggested by the fact that on 7 April 1871 the Illinois Railroad Act was passed because of pressure from the Grangers; this act created a railroad commission with the power to fix maximum rates and prohibit discriminations. Similar legislation was passed in 1874 in Wisconsin and Iowa. The relationship between the farmer and the railroads was that of customer to supplier, but the customer needed the supplier to get his perishable foodstuffs to market even more than the supplier needed the customer's business; the result was that the farmer was at the mercy of the railroads so far as rates were concerned. Many farmers and former farmers must have felt that the James boys were fighting their enemy when they interfered with the railroads.

I do not intend to argue that the James gang was actually in the business of social reform. Doubtless all the banking and railroading activity that I have been talking about merely provided an opportunity for depredation which Jesse's ingenuity was not long in taking advantage of. But the surrounding social and economic conditions were such that the Missouri farmers among whom the Jameses and Youngers lived would have felt a thrill of vengeful glee when they heard the news of a bank or train robbery. These feelings would have led them to make heroes out of the robbers.

But why Jesse James? The first group of causes which we have discussed would apply to any criminal, and undoubtedly these causes applied to a good many minor figures whose reputations have not survived their trials. The second group of causes would apply exceptionally well to Jesse James, for while sources are divided as to whether Jesse actually invented the bank robbery and the train robbery, certainly he was among the first two or three bank robbers and train robbers in America and equally certainly brought both arts to a high state of perfection; but, while Jesse's activities would make him especially likely to be remembered in view of the attitudes toward banks and trains which prevailed during the first decade after the Civil War, the activities of many other robbers would also make them only slightly less likely to appeal to the popular imagination. Yet who today remembers Poke Wells? Why, when no one remembers the perpetrators of the Brookfield bank holdup about which the whole country was talking in 1882, are the name and fame of Jesse James still alive?

To begin with, and most obviously, there is the fortuitous happenstance that his name alliterates. We have long known that alliteration is a factor in memory retention, and Jesse James is rhythmically alliterative. It would be much harder to forget the name of Jesse James than, for example, Butch Cassidy, Cole Younger, or, for that matter, Frank James.

There are other elements of the James legend which operated in favor of its survival. At the time, there was the fact that Jesse and his gang eluded capture for years; but this motif is not stressed in the survival of the legend into our own day, and it is not mentioned in the ballad. Another factor which may have contributed to the legend is the suspicion that Jesse James did not die but survived as J. Frank Dalton or any one of a number of other claimants; but, while there was much contemporary suspicion that the body exhibited in 1882 was not that of Jesse James, it is more likely that the legend caused the claims than that the claimants caused the legend.

More germane to an explanation of this survival is the fact that Jesse was assassinated. As a leader cut down in his prime, he obviously joins the ranks of martyred heroes with whom he has nothing else in common—Abraham Lincoln, John F. Kennedy, Martin Luther King, Robert F. Kennedy. As the case of James A. Garfield makes clear, assassination is not enough to ensure apotheosis; but when it is combined with other elements, it can give legend a powerful impetus. Moreover, there is an inherent structural irony in the story: Jesse was assassinated by one of his own band, who betrayed him for a reward. If I were forced to put my finger on one single factor which, more than any other one, contributed to the endurance of the James legend, I would select the dramatic irony of the fact that it was one of his own confederates and comrades who killed him. The analogue to this is too well known to need specifying; one suspects that it was for a good, though subliminal, reason that Woody Guthrie chose the tune of the Jesse James song for his "Ballad of Jesus Christ."

The question with which we began was why Jesse James grew into a hero in the American folk imagination. My answer is that there is a fortuitous combination of circumstances. Some of these circumstances are inseparable from his profession; there are good reasons why any bandit may seem like a Robin Hood, as he robs from the rich if he is efficient at all, and gives to the poor since once he has money the only thing to do with it is spend it lavishly. Other circumstances relate to historical causes, such as Jesse's attacks on banks and railroads at a time when both institutions were highly unpopular in Jesse's part of the country, as indeed in rural America generally—banks because they foreclosed on unpaid mortgages, and railroads because they had the farmer's land condemned for what he thought was less than its worth and then charged him what he considered exorbitant rates to get his produce to market. And still others derived from specific incidents in Jesse's career, especially his archetypal assassination by a trusted confederate. The combination seems sufficient to assure his immortality in the American mind.

FROM

COLLECTED POEMS

By Max Douglas

1978

The True Story of the Death of Charlie Ford

One morning
Charlie Ford & I
startd to the timber

to hunt squirrels.
As we were going across the barn lot,
Charlie made an excuse to go back to the house.

Then I heard a shot—
Charlie Ford did not shoot himself
to death in a weed patch, as has bn told so many times.

(End of Cycle)

FROM

SPEECHES AND WRITINGS OF WM. H. WALLACE

By William H. Wallace

1914

For fifteen years after the close of the Civil War the "Missouri outlaws," generally known as the "James Boys," terrorized our Commonwealth. Seven years of this time was while the Republicans held offices in the State. Eight years while they were held by the Democrats. During this fifteen years the newspapers of the nation teemed with accounts of their depredations. Probably two-thirds of their depredations were within the borders of Missouri. The other one-third extended from Alabama to Minnesota and from West Virginia to Kansas. The plain truth should be told. These outlaws robbed citizens, stage coaches, banks, railroad trains, express companies and others. They killed citizens, bank cashiers, railroad conductors, laborers, detectives and officers. The band usually consisted of six men. At one time, when they went to Northfield, Minnesota, it numbered eight. During the fifteen years above named about twenty-two men belonged to it. Most of them died with their boots on. Several of them were killed by their own comrades. When one was killed a new recruit was put in his place.

These outlaws held the people of Missouri in absolute terror. It was thought to mean death to report on them. They had stopping places in Jackson, Clay, Ray, Lafayette, Johnson and elsewhere, but no man dared to say he had seen them. The wife of Tucker Bassham, who was placed in the penitentiary for train robbery in connection with the band at Glendale, Mo., told me that Jesse James said at her table that he would kill a woman who informed on them just as quickly as he would a man. The following story was told Judge H. P. White by a Confederate soldier: "A bank had been robbed in Jackson County. A man who knew the perpetrators was summoned before the grand jury. He gave them all the facts and names. When being excused he said, 'Gentlemen, I have told the truth. I will never swear a lie,' and drawing a pistol, he said, 'the notches on this pistol give the number of men I have killed. My life is now in danger and I desire to say that if anybody is indicted each man on this grand jury can dig his grave.' No one was indicted."

The damage done to Missouri was incalculable. Missouri was regarded as their home, and the truth is, as a rule it was, and the people had to suffer the stigma of their deeds. The greatest injury was to the good name of the grand old Commonwealth and her people. Ninety-nine one hundredths of the citizens of our State disapproved of the crimes of these bandits, but all suffered the shame alike. Missourians as cultured and moral as any people in the Union did not have the standing in the nation which they deserved. Many regarded them as ruffians in sympathy with train robbery and murder—people who gave food and shelter to bandits. The *Globe-Democrat*, a great daily published at St. Louis, for more than a decade constantly referred to these robberies and homicides continually crying out, "Poor old Missouri." A newspaper up in Iowa suggested that Missouri be called the "Robber State." The press of the Union took it up and for more than ten years this appellation was applied to our blessed Commonwealth. I am not exaggerating one particle. Every man who lived in Missouri thirty years ago knows I am telling the exact truth.

The injury to the State from the standpoint of economics was almost as great as that to its good name. Capital did not come to the State as it should have come. Land in Missouri is now worth fully as much as similar land in Iowa. Then the Iowa land was worth twice as much, although Iowa was younger than Missouri. Homeseekers passed through Missouri and bought land in Kansas, paying double as much as they could have bought better land for in Missouri.

It was during this epoch in the history of our State, when the great body of law-abiding Southerners as well as Northerners became tired of outlawry and began to look for officers willing to aid in suppressing it, that I became a candidate for prosecuting attorney in 1880. It was the constant contention of the friends of the James Boys that they did not commit these depredations; that they "were being lied on," and many of them were honest in their contention. When in 1876 the news came of the awful tragedy of the attempted bank robbery at Northfield, Minn., a splendid Christian lady who was my client and at whose home the outlaws often stopped, came to my office in Independence and said to me, "Well, I see they are lying on the boys again." She was astonished when I told her the pictures in the St. Louis dailies were the pictures of the boys, some of them her near relatives. She knew I knew some of their faces well. There were hundreds of splendid people who believed just as she did.

Before going farther I wish to say that I have not the slightest feeling of enmity for any one of the Missouri outlaws or any of their friends. For years I have numbered among their relatives and defenders some of my warmest friends. If any one of them entertains the slightest ill will toward me I do not know it. Without exception they are accustomed to say that I was under oath, that I fought them out in the open and at no time was ever guilty of the least unfairness or underhandedness. I wish to put in the record, too, what I can truthfully say in their favor.

Frank and Jesse James, though outlaws, had families, and I believe were true to them. I knew Frank James' wife before he married her. She is a splendid woman. They have a son, who, I believe, was a soldier

Harold Dillinger Collection

Prosecutor William H. Wallace

beneath the Stars and Stripes in the Spanish war. I wish Frank James well and I have often told him so when I have met him since his trial at Gallatin. I met him at Dallas, Texas, after the trial at Gallatin. He said he would like it if he and I would speak to each other when we met. I told him I had tried my levelest to hang him but could not, and was willing to speak to him, and hoped he would make of himself a good citizen. Thirty long years have elapsed since the jury acquitted him, and I do not believe that during that time he has ever committed an unlawful act. Nor do I entertain the slightest hatred toward the memory of Jesse James. I have always denounced his assassination as one of the most cowardly and damnable deeds in all history. I did not know his wife, but from what I heard of her, I believed her to be a good and true woman. I know his son, Jesse James, Jr., a lawyer at the Kansas City Bar, very well, always speak to him and certainly wish him an honorable and successful career. I entertain the most kindly feeling for Coleman Younger. A short time before he was pardoned I wrote an earnest letter to the Governor of Minnesota saying that I thought that after the lapse of 25 years the time for mercy had come and asking his release. I think Cole Younger has kept his pledge and conducted himself as a good citizen. I say this much of these men because justice and humanity suggest it . . .

But to return to my narrative and look at the situation a few months after Ryan was convicted. The following was now the situation with reference to the six members of the band as given by Dick Liddil. Liddil himself had surrendered. Charlie Ford, who was never in but one robbery according to Liddil, had also come in. Liddil said Bob had never belonged to the band, although he became acquainted with the members of the band at the Ford farm. Jesse James, Wood Hite and Ed. Miller had been killed by their own comrades. Bill Ryan and Clarence Hite were in the penitentiary. The band was overthrown. Only Frank James was yet an outlaw, and he had a $10,000 reward offered by the Governor hanging over his head.

At this juncture two ladies came to my office one day. One of them was a large old lady with an empty sleeve—the only one-armed lady I ever saw. I had never seen her before. The face of the other lady was hidden by a thick veil. The older lady said they wished to see me in my private office. When the door was closed the lady with the veil removed it and asked me if I knew her. I told her it had been a good many years since I saw her, but I certainly did; that she was Annie Ralston, who I now understood was Frank James's wife. She said I was correct. She said she had come to propose to have Frank, her husband, surrender to me; that they were very much afraid he would be killed for the reward while in the act of giving himself up. She said they were satisfied I had nothing to do with the killing of Jesse James and they were willing to have Frank surrender to me, believing I would protect him. I remember my words to her at the time. I said, "Mrs. James, if your husband surrenders to me, if he is harmed it will be over my dead body." I told her, however, that I did not believe she ought to refuse to trust the other officers; that I did not believe that any officer had caused the death of Jesse James; that I believed that the Fords out of their own wickedness, and in order get the reward, had killed Jesse James of their own motion. She said Frank was living in perfect torment; that with a $10,000 reward on his head "he could not even cut a stick of wood without looking around to see whether or not some one was slipping up behind him to kill him." She wanted to know what the terms of surrender would be. I told her I would have to consult the Governor as I could only agree as to offenses committed in Jackson County. I immediately telegraphed the Governor, who telegraphed back that he would let me name the terms. It was the nearest I have ever came to being governor. I sent word to Mrs. James that the State could not agree that her husband could go absolutely free, but if he would give himself up and end the whole matter the State would be satisfied with a short term in the penitentiary. In a day or two the reply came that my proposal would not be accepted.

In a short time I received a telegram from the Governor stating that Frank James had given himself up to him, and that he was sending him to Independence to be delivered into my custody. I met Frank James at Independence and turned him over to the county marshal, Cornelius Murphy, the proper custodian. A great crowd had assembled at Independence to see Frank James. His friends from Jackson and other counties were there in great numbers. The question of bail at once came up. It was said that James had friends there worth over a million dollars ready to go on his bail, and I think this was true. But the indictment against him at Independence, written by a prosecutor ahead of me, was for murder in the first degree, which, under our law, is not bailable without a showing. When I was asked to consent to bail I replied, as of course I was compelled to do, that I was under oath and could not agree to bail without a showing. Of course they could not make such a showing as Frank denied that he knew anything about the crime with which he was charged. Major John N. Edwards, a talented newspaper editor—known from his style as the "Victor Hugo" of the West—and a great friend of Frank James, asked me to one side in the Merchants Hotel at Independence, and said if I would consent to Frank James's being admitted to bail it would make me the most popular man in the State; it would make me governor, and he would be glad to do all he could to bring this about. I remember my exact reply to him to this day. I said, "Major, I would like to be governor, but I am on oath, and it comes too high."

About this time there was a Democratic convention to nominate county officers, including prosecuting attorney. The friends of the Jameses and the lawless classes in Kansas City were opposing me most vehemently, but I made no effort to be nominated, and asked no one to support me. I stayed in court at Kansas City trying cases until the day the convention met at Independence, which I attended, simply saying that they could do as they pleased about nominating me; that I stood on my record. When nominations for prosecuting attorney were called for, there were outcries against me. I went forward to the platform and withdrew from the contest, stating that I did not wish the nomination as there seemed to be opposition to me. The other candidates then made their pleas for the nomination, and the voting began. As ward after ward in Kansas City and township after township out in the country was called they voted for me until I had almost every vote in the convention, and when it was moved to make it unanimous one delegate cried out, "No." I went forward and began to make a speech, declining, when friends rushed to me and insisted that it was my duty to accept and finish the work I had commenced as prosecutor. I sat down and was declared the nominee.

The friends of Frank James came to me, wanting to know whether I intended to prosecute or let him go. I told them it would be my duty to prosecute him to the full extent of my ability. Then the storm commenced. I had, if anything, a hotter time than I had had two years before. A committee of Frank James' friends, ex-Guerrillas, followed me all over the county in my canvass. I did not know for what, but I supposed in an effort to intimidate me. I recall a meeting one night at Independence. The court room was packed. While I was pleading for the good name of the State and denouncing outlawry, as I did everywhere, a friend of Frank James, an ex-Guerrilla, said to be a dead shot, arose and interrupted me. I supposed it meant a pre-concerted plan to intimidate me, and I fired into him with all the vehemence at my command. He came back at me vehemently, but I had the advantage of having the floor. By this time the crowd was standing in their seats yelling furiously. The chairman, a two hundred and twenty-five pound banker, slipped up to me and said, "For God's sake let up. There will be blood shed here in less than a minute." I told him that if he was afraid he could leave; that I believed I could take care of that crowd without a chairman. A few seconds afterwards I looked around to where he had been sitting as chairman and he was gone. He had slipped out of a side door, and I was both speaker and chairman. Some one in the back end of the court room cried, "Take him out." I said, "There is another coward and friend of train robbers," and dared him to come forward and try it on. After a while quiet was restored, and I finished my speech. The next morning a prominent physician, and a regular ex-Confederate, Dr. Jackson, came smiling to me on the street and said, "That was a terrible tongue lashing you gave me last night." I replied that I certainly had not done so. He said, "Yes, you did"; that he was the fellow that hallooed, "Take him out," but he did not mean to take me out but the man who was interrupting me. I finished my race and was re-elected.

I began now to prepare for the Frank James trial, which commenced in August, 1883, at Gallatin, Daviess County, Missouri. He was charged with murder in the first degree in the killing of Frank McMillan, while engaged in a train robbery at Winston, Mo., on July 5, 1881. I will not encumber this account by detailing the evidence. All of the evidence on both sides is correctly given in my Frank James speech published in this book, which, as we lawyers say, I beg leave to introduce and have considered as "Exhibit A." I traveled thousands of miles in collecting the evidence for the State. The State, in my judgment, had an overwhelming case—more than twice as strong as the case against Bill Ryan. There are just a few outside circumstances which ought briefly to be stated.

As the trial came on I was sitting at Gallatin in front of the office of Mr. Hamilton, the prosecuting attorney of Daviess County. I noticed the sheriff, who was summoning the jury, standing in the courthouse yard. The town was full of people. He would pull a paper out of his pocket, look at it and then go across the street and accost some man standing on the sidewalk, and then come back into the courthouse yard, take the paper out of his pocket and go through the same performance. I went over to where he was. I told him I was satisfied we were going to have a packed jury. He wanted to know why. I told him I had been watching him; that he had a list of jurors in his pocket which had been prepared before hand. He said he was getting a good jury. I reminded him that he had promised me to go out into the county and get a good honest jury. He said he intended to get a good jury without going to the country. I went back and told Mr. Hamilton, the prosecuting attorney, a courageous, splendid young fellow, what had occurred. He and I agreed to join in an affidavit alleging improper conduct on the part of Crozier, the sheriff, the man above referred to, and asking that he be deposed by the court and the coroner, a gentleman named Claggett, be directed to summons the jury as the law provided in such cases. This was strenuously objected to by others interested in the prosecution. They said the coroner was an ex-Confederate soldier and it would never do to have an ex-Confederate select the jury. I did not know Mr. Claggett, and I said, "Is he honest?" They replied that he was; that he was quiet and honest, and they did not know that he had ever expressed an opinion, but that he was an ex-Confederate. I told them that I had been in the fight against the James boys for nearly three years and that the ex-Confederates had been in the van for the overthrow of the

James boys from the very start. I said, let's have the ex-Confederate. The town was packed with the friends of Frank James from many parts of the country. The news spread as to what Hamilton and I intended to do, and they were perfectly furious. They had no idea of permitting an ex-Confederate to select a jury to try Frank James if by any means they could prevent it. The excitement was intense. The air was full of threats of violence. The judge, hearing of the situation, came over to Hamilton's office and wanted to know if Hamilton and I intended to swear Sheriff Crozier off. He said if we did there would certainly be blood shed. We told him there was nothing else to do; that justice was being cheated. The judge then said, "Gentlemen, I am not in the habit of announcing my decisions beforehand, but if you file such a motion I will certainly overrule it in order to prevent bloodshed."

I went down to my hotel; packed my grip; brought it up to Hamilton's office, and told my associates that I was going home. They said that I had been in the fight and knew all the evidence while they did not, and it would be improper to desert them and leave them to conduct a case which they did not understand. I told them that if they put it on that ground I would stay, but they must bear in mind that we would simply try Frank James before the world; that the verdict of the jury, being selected, was already written.

I ought to add that there probably never was a trial where there was so much talk about "honor," "duels," "shooting on sight" and so forth as in this one, and I seemed to be the hapless victim of all the intended vengeance, although I have never done anything except to look up the law and the evidence and push the prosecution. One chivalric gentleman, against whom I had never spoken an unkind word, wrote out a challenge inviting me to the "field of honor," and handed it to his second, but upon being told by a gentleman in the room that he had heard me say that if I was challenged I would have the challenger arrested under the statute; called his second back and tore it up. I had said that I thought it took more courage to decline or ignore a challenge than to accept one, and I think so yet. Another distinguished gentleman, whom I had never harmed and against whom I had never uttered a word, challenged me to the deadly field, and published his challenge in the paper of Dr. Morrison Mumford, the Kansas City Times, but I was out of Kansas City at the time, and before I heard of it Dick Liddil accepted it, but the challenger refused to fight Liddil on the ground that "he was no gentleman." The trial of Frank James was a long one, and to get a little fresh air to help me bear the tremendous strain of the contest I was accustomed to take a horseback ride out in the country by myself after the adjournment of court in the evening. Just as I was starting one evening Dr. Black, a prominent citizen of Gallatin, came up and told me that not two minutes before he had heard a noted shooter say he intended to kill me on sight, and Black begged me to put up my horse and go to my room in the hotel. I told him they were trying to scare me out of town, but, even if they were in earnest, the surest plan for me to get shot was to begin to run. I took my ride that evening, and continued to take it until the case ended. The reader must not think I am making any special claim to courage. I may have been scared into reasonable boldness, thinking this was the safest plan.

Frank James was acquitted. I had him brought back to Kansas City, intending to try him on an indictment for robbing a C. & A. train at Blue Cut in Jackson County, September 7, 1881. It would have been impossible for Frank James to have escaped on this indictment, for I had fully as strong a case as for the Winston robbery, for which he was tried at Gallatin, and Cornelius Murphy, who summoned the jury that convicted Bill Ryan, was still in office and would have summoned a jury to try Frank James. M. M. Langhorne, Amazon Hays and Whig Keshlaer would have assisted and been on guard just as they were in the Ryan trial. But there was much doubt as to the legality of Liddil's testimony, and it was much talked of throughout the State. Liddil had been placed in the penitentiary before he joined the James Band and his pardon being only issued under the three-fourths rule it was claimed he was incompetent as a witness. Liddil's testimony had been strenuously opposed at Gallatin, but Judge Goodman overruled the objection. While Frank James was in jail at Independence, awaiting trial for the Blue Cut robbery, Judge T. A.

Sherwood, of the Missouri Supreme Court, handed down an opinion in the case of State vs. Grant, a negro whom I had convicted for murder in the first degree for killing Patrick Jones, a policeman. In this case, see State vs. Grant, 79 Mo., 113. Judge Sherwood held that one Miller, a witness for the State, who had been convicted of petit larceny, was not competent to testify. The opinion was a very lengthy one, and every lawyer who read it said at once, "That disqualifies Wallace's witness, Dick Liddil," and it did just as specifically as if it had been written in the Frank James case. I asked the Governor to issue a full pardon to Liddil, restoring his competency. The Governor refused. There was nothing left for me to do except to dismiss the case, which I did.

Thus ended the career of the Missouri outlaws. Probably no bandit band in history came to a more ignominious ending. Only Frank James escaped. Tucker Bassham served a term in the penitentiary. Ed Miller, Liddil says, was killed by Jesse James and left lying in the road in Saline County. Clarence Hite was placed in the penitentiary for twenty-five years, pardoned and died shortly afterward with consumption. Bill Ryan was placed in the penitentiary for twenty-five years, served seven years and was pardoned by Governor Morehouse. Wood Hite was killed by Bob Ford and Dick Liddil. Jesse James was killed by Bob and Charlie Ford at St. Joseph, Mo. Dick Liddil gave himself up and became a witness for the State. He afterwards died and was buried at Independence. Charlie Ford, borne down, it was said, with disease and remorse, committed suicide in a weed patch. Bob Ford, a helper, though never a regular member of the band, was killed in a saloon at Creede, Colo.

Jesse James Farm & Museum, Kearney, Missouri

Jesse's mother, Zerelda, at his grave, circa 1900. His wife, whose voice Arthur Winfield Knight appropriated for the poem on the facing page, was also named Zerelda.

FROM

WANTED!

By Arthur Winfield Knight

1988

Zerelda James: At Jesse's Grave

Never mind the rain.
Jesse can't feel it now
and I can wipe it away,
the way I do my tears.
If I could just wipe away
the other things . . .

I told Jesse
not to trust the Ford boys,
but he said they were kin.
I told Jesse
never to turn his back.
There were omens in the sky
that day. Jesse's head
rested in a pool of blood

brighter than a cardinal,
but no birds sang.

I tell you this:
Jesse was murdered
by a coward whose name
is not worthy to appear here.

I could not have asked
for a more loving husband
nor a more caring father
for my children.

I tell you:
I stayed awake
a lot of nights
fretting
when Jesse was away;
I'd listen to the cicadas:
"Jesse will be home tonight,
Jesse will be home tonight,"
but I always knew
that wasn't true.

I've spent a lifetime pretending.

FROM

MISSOURI BITTERSWEET

By MacKinlay Kantor

1969

"Jesse James was a lad who killed many a man—"

Jesse didn't really want to kill nobody. The murders attributed to him were committed by bandits other than Jesse. He was kind of like Lancelot or Galahad or Jolly Robin—real nice. When he slew at all, he slew as a knightly duty whilst riding in support of the Lost Cause, suh.

Jesse was the brains of the James gang. His brother Frank was the strong-arm boy, the goon, the gunner.

Frank James dreamed up all the plots about who and what to rob, and where; but Frank was wishy-washy at heart, and it took a real tough guy like Jesse to command.

The Younger brothers—Cole, Jim, Bob, et al—persuaded those decent forthright honest James brothers into banditry.

It was the James boys who were the original Bad Company, and the Youngers were bedazzled by them into a life of crime.

"Jesse robbed from the rich, and he gave unto the poor—"

He never gave away a nickel in his life. He was tough and

mean, but stupid. If he hadn't been plain born stupid he wouldn't have taken off his guns on April 3rd, 1882, and thus permitted Bobby Ford to take a crack at him.

Jesse James was smart as tacks.

"He was a great big tall man. Oh, taller than—Taller than—"

"My grandpa knew Jesse real well. He said he was just about ordinary-sized."

"Jesse was kind of on the small side. What my Granmaw always said. And she had good reason to remember him. Cause one time the mortgage on her place was due, and she didn't have no money, and she was crying. Then along come a band of men riding right up this here lane, and they says, 'Lady, we ain't gonna harm you, but we're right hungry, and need something to eat. So will you please trot us out some dinner.' Well, Granmaw give em what she had, and they et, and then, when they was about to leave, Jesse—for it was him, in person—he asked Granmaw what she had been crying about. She up and tolt him, and he left a pile of gold pieces right there on the kitchen table, for her to pay the mortgage with. Long towards evening here comes Mr. Caleb Sniggs from the bank in town, and he says, 'Drucie—' He'd knowed Granmaw all her young life, so he called her by name—'Drucie,' he says, 'I know you hain't got the money, so I'm gonna have to foreclose.' She says, calm and firm, 'I have too got the money, every cent of it. Here tis, and you kindly hand over that mortgage paper.' Well, was old Sniggs mad and angry, for he'd planned to get this here farm for his own self, see? But by that time Granpaw had come in from plowing corn, and he cast an eye towards his Forty-four-forty—There tis, same gun, right up there on them brackets. So there wasn't nothing for Caleb Sniggs to do but hand over them mortgage papers, and Granmaw and Granpaw burnt em, right there in the fireplace, before his very eyes. Old Sniggs started off towards town in his buggy. Pretty soon there's an almighty row down the road, with shots and yelling, and, fore you could say Uncle-Speck-go-spit-on-the-stove, old Caleb Sniggs come running up the lane, fast as he could pelt. You know what? Jesse James and his outlaws had laid in wait for that there banker, and they'd stole *back* all them twenty-dollar gold pieces that Jesse'd give to my Granmaw. They took along his horse and buggy, too. I tell you, that's the kind of man Jesse James really *was*. And that's all the pure truth, and it happened just like that, right here on this place."

Jesse's father was a preacher, and Jesse learned to read and write when very young; and when falsely accused of crimes later on, he wrote voluminous letters to the Kansas City *Times*, extenuating himself.

Those Kansas City *Times* letters were written by an alcoholic newspaperman, John Newman Edwards. Jesse himself was illiterate.

Jesse had a *mother* whose name was Zerelda, but she was known as Zee.

Jesse's *wife* was named Zerelda. Commonly called Zee.

(Pshaw. Both were Zereldas.)

Jesse wore a full beard, most times.

Jesse usually sported a mustache.

Jesse was always clean-shaven, except when he went disguised as "Mr. Howard."

From one end of Missouri to the other there exist multiple caverns, and many of the caves are open to the public on payment of a fee. (Once in a while you find a free cave off the beaten track, but those farmers are beginning to get the word.) In a good half of the caves a wide rock will be pointed out to you; and behind that rock the James boys lay in ambush, and shot the Pinkerton detectives when they came in. In the other half the Pinkerton men lay in ambush, and shot it out with the Jameses. But, either way, it was the Pinkerton men who got killed in the end.

(Thus far no serious student of the Jesse James saga has found a record of any such cave or any such encounter.)

But the legends keep growing, like grainy brainy tan mushrooms which rise in moist woodland every spring. They are old, they are new, they shrink, they expand, they can be dried for future use. And, like those same April morels or like autumn thorn-apples, they taste good when you bite into them, be they fanciful myths or no.

Along about fifty-five years ago a hard-faced man with pale tobacco-stained handlebar mustachios came driving his van into our little prairie town, and parked it alongside John Richardson's jewelry store at the corner of Second Street and Willson Avenue. Carefully he set brakes against all four wheels of the van, which was bedizened with exciting signs. The largest of these read: *See Jesse James. In Person. Admission 25¢, Children 10¢.* We boys followed along, after Mr. Handlebar had unhitched his team, and by bicycle we escorted him to Filloon's livery barn where his fine black Percherons became star boarders for the next couple of days. We used to sneak in there and watch the team munching their dinner. It was a thrill just to observe them; they were a *foreign* team—"Missouri bred and foaled," their owner declared between expectorations.

So was Jesse James. In that glorious pink-painted van he reposed in an absolutely terrifying coffin, clad in the exact costume which Jesse wore the day when the Dirty Little Coward shot him (so said the proprietor). Also displayed were Bobby Ford's gun; Jesse's own revolvers; ropes used to hang the Bald Knobbers in 1889; Daniel Boone's rifle—"Old Tick-Licker"; Daniel Boone's very own coonskin cap; an alleged two-headed calf in alcohol; an alleged three-headed colt; copperheads, rattlesnakes, "the only hoopsnake every captured alive in the Ozark Mountains"—but by now it too was dead and all tangled and twisted in a five-gallon jar. There were front and rear steps, and you came in at the rear and went out at the front. (Reluctantly.) I wasted my substance on Mr. Handlebar's portable museum. I collected the regular weekly dollar for carrying my *Freeman-Tribune* paper route, gave Mother the prescribed twenty-five cents which was Mackie's token contribution to our family budget, and spent *sixty cents* in worshiping beside Jesse James' bier. I would have spent seventy cents, except that the curfew blew and I had to go home.

I wasn't the only one, either. At seven o'clock Saturday night the line extended around a corner and all the way up to Alfred Rasmussen's shoe store. The old Missourian—the live one—had a way of saying, "Show's over. Lecture's over. Next show starts in five minutes," and shooing the public out the front door, no matter how much we longed to linger. It cost another dime to get back in, when our turns finally came again. . . .Truly, I have visited many museums over the world which afforded less macabre satisfaction. Take catacombs and crypts, whether in Paris or Rome or Naples . . . Jesse James had them beat by a mile. He wasn't just a wad of bones or a dummy, not by a dang sight. He was a man—real, dead, dried up, kind of mummified. Mr. Handlebar Mustache would open Jesse's coat, pull up his shirt, and show you the cross-hatched stitching on that brown parchment hide where the *viscera* had been removed. They took out his—" (lowered voice)—"guts; yes, them doctors did. Claimed they wanted to find out what made him so mean. But I reckon they never did find out." Jesse's face had been reconstructed with wax, so the boss was forced to admit that the beard was false as well.

Fearful and wonderful the moment wherein a large key was produced . . . the proprietor would reach into the coffin, twist the key through a powerful amount of clicking, and set in motion some cranial clockworks whereby the staring glass eyes of Jesse James began to open . . . shut . . . open . . . shut . . . until the mechanism ran down.

"Folks'll try to tell you that after Jesse was kilt, they put his body on a train, and tuck it over to Mrs. Samuel's place—that was his Ma—and buried it in her front yard. They had a real bang-up funeral, and I reckon even Governor Crittenden come to pay his respects. But twasn't Jesse who was lying in that grave. Twas a poor tramp who got knifed in a fight down by the railroad tracks in St. Jo, same day that Bobby Ford come a sneaking and a-murdering. Some friends of Jesse's—my own brother Claiborne was one of em—was fearful that maybe the enemies of Jesse James would dig up his corpse in the dark of the moon, and cut it up, and sell the pieces for souvenirs. So they carried his body to a place of safety, and nobody else knew any different. That's how come that I am now enabled to exhibit before your very eyes the positively genuine body of the one and only Jesse Woodson James, treacherously slain by Robert Judas Iscariot Ford for the sake of thirty pieces of silver. . . . Speaking of silver—Come on now. Everybody out! Lecture's over! Next show begins in five minutes."

He drove his brawny Percherons and the lumbering van west on a long road toward Fort Dodge, come Sunday morning. A posse of small boys rode herd on him for a way—then we turned back: too many mud-holes. An hour afterward I put in my required appearance at the Baptist Sunday School, where our teacher talked endearingly about *David, the son of Jesse*. You can imagine just which Jesse that conjured up . . . an annoyed ghost on a phantom horse, stalking that pink portable museum all the way to Fort Dodge and farther. Even at such early age I recognized that the Jesse James corpse, relics and tales were all a lot of rubbish, fascinating though they might have been. I didn't think that any man who robbed the Gallatin bank, stopped the Glendale train, shot Captain Sheets to the ground, and went to his rest with his hand on his breast—"the Devil will be upon his knee"—No such man would take all that hogwash lying down. In eerie dreams I saw him spurring his horse alongside Mr. Handlebar with menace and profanity; but still I doubted that the old rapscallion might see or feel Jesse James in the wind.

He's been dead going on ninety years. Yet you can sniff him in surviving hedgerows and wild crabapple trees, and see him running with lies or loot above the fields of hybrid corn—say Pioneer, Single Cross, 3306. (Conforming corn, never imagined by people who cultivated the ragged fields of Jesse's time.)

Clay County, where he was born, is today mostly a squeezed carton of ranchhouses, swimming pools, parking lots, motels, filling stations, supermarkets . . . Kansas City suburbs, with Interstate 35 booming off toward the north; and U.S. 69, nearly as swollen with traffic, fired like a string of noisy bullets toward Excelsior Springs and back again.

Jackson County, immediately to the south, is more of the same. It retains only a few tiny corners where there's room enough for a bird to perch or silence enough for him to sing in. Farther south, in the old guerrilla country of Cass, Bates, Vernon and adjoining counties, there are still extant the farms and villages which one time knew the pressure of Jesse James' feet or the squeak of his stirrups. Also up north of the Big Muddy in Carroll, Ray, Caldwell, and over across Daviess and De Kalb into Andrew County and Buchanan, where he died . . . there stand certain deserted farm houses which were packed with busy breathing humans when Jesse was a-riding and a-robbing . . . now tenanted only by bats, and swallows and wasps building their own odd cottages in corners of the sagging porches and privies.

MAG, Page 292:

> The Jesse James house . . . is a small, one-story frame cottage, recently moved to its present location from 1318 LaFayette Street and operated as a tourist attraction. . . . Here the outlaw . . . lived quietly with his family as a respected, mild-mannered citizen known as "Mr. Howard." And here, on April 5, 1882, [Sic. This would seem to be a misprint. The correct date, April 3, is given on page 514] he was killed by a former lieutenant, Bob Ford, assisted by his brother Charles, who wanted the $10,000 reward. Mrs. James swore out a warrant charging them with the murder of her husband. The men were sentenced to be hanged but were pardoned by Governor T. T. Crittenden. They were subsequently released from another charge of murder in Ray County. According to early accounts, after receiving the reward, they lived in debauchery until Charles committed suicide and Robert was shot in a Colorado dance hall.

I have had neither time nor inclination to pursue Bobby's post–J. J.-murder career down the byways of Evil Americana. But anecdote relates that, when Ford was murdered, the killer offered his motive for the crime. "He wanted to kill the man who killed Jesse James." The anecdote progresses: Bobby Ford's killer was in turn killed by a man who wanted to be the man who killed the man who killed Jesse James. As I say, this is unsupported anecdote. Just how long might that domino-soldier technique have continued?

The Howard cottage is little more than a shack, but in 1938 there came an attempt to move it to the World's Fair which would open the next year in New York. Mr. Walter Meierhoffer, Sr., then president of the Chamber of Commerce, did not wish to see the house taken away from St. Jo. He bought it himself, and hauled the cottage down to the Belt Highway. I hear as how a Mr. George Miller owns it now.

Maybe he owns also the place next door. JESSE JAMES ULTRA-MODERN MOTEL. WELCOME SALESMEN AND TRUCKERS. There are a couple of antique buggies out in the yard, and some handsome locust trees grow beside the house itself. MUSEUM OPEN DAILY. WHERE JESSE JAMES WAS KILLED. SEE THE BULLET HOLE.

The attendant is charming—Edna Martin, a widow of middle years with a calm manner and an honest Missouri accent. If you want to buy any of the tourist junk which is for sale in a room alongside the death chamber, Mrs. Martin will be glad to wait on you. I suspect that she enjoys much more the business of discussing the death of Jesse James, and in authentic language.

I told her that I remembered the old wallpaper from years ago. Tan, with a little blue splotching on it—

"It's the same. So are all these pictures of Jesse, both alive and dead, hanging around the room. And that's the same 'God Bless Our Home' motto up there on the wall—"

"Some say that he was hanging up the motto when Ford shot him, others say that he was taking it down. Which is correct?"

"Neither one. He was straightening it. It was crooked, and he wanted to set it right. The Ford brothers had come here, and he trusted them, although Bobby was a new recruit in the gang, and hadn't yet participated in anything big. They were out for that ten-thousand-dollar reward, pure and simple, but Jesse never had a notion about it. His guns were heavy and uncomfortable, so he took off his guns and put them on the sofa over there. When he climbed up on a chair to reach for the motto, Bobby shot him in the back of the head. The bullet came out near his left eye and went into the wall."

"That's where they've got the glass over the old bullet hole?"

"Yes, people were always digging out chunks of the plaster, or cutting off tiny bits of wallpaper. That's how it got to be such a big hole. So finally the glass was put over it so's they couldn't work any more ruination. . . . We don't have too many personal items that were actually in the house in 1882. There's some old lamps, and those pictures of Jesse's children. And here's some marbles that the children used to play with—at least the marbles were found in the house after Jesse's wife and children were gone. And here's the frame of his mother's spectacles . . . this is an old platter which came from his mother's house . . . "

I looked into the back bedroom allegedly occupied by the pretended Mr. Howard and his wife the night before he died. Nothing in there but a cheap bed with a blue-and-white comforter over it. I wondered whether the Jameses made love in that bed, or on one like it, during the early morning of April 3rd. Many J. J. buffs insist that Zee was beautiful, and that Jesse loved her with devotion.

The whole place seemed pathetic, lower-rustic-middle-class, shop-worn, trivial—a let-down after fierce gunfights and front-page banditry. If there should exist any survival of the human entity (Uncle Mack hain't witnessed no evidence of such survival to date) it is difficult to believe that Jesse would be hanging around there, with Belt Highway traffic howling its head off a few rods away, and a gas station promising JESSE JAMES SUPER SERVICE. REGULAR 22 CENTS.

Well, they may have had some J. J. candy for sale in that next room, along with the souvenirs, but I couldn't force myself to go in there.

You can feel more of Jesse James when you look at an abandoned right-of-way where a train groaned through prairie night until the bandits stopped it. Or in riding the same ravines where their horses whickered. Or in listening to a banjo or a guitar strummed beside a fire, and hearing Billy Gashade's song sung as it should be sung. Or in wondering what ancient revolver shots go echoing still, far through other space and other dimensions, even though neon signs now glow in all too many dark places previously sacred to the katydids.

FROM

THE JESSE JAMES POEMS

By Paulette Jiles

1988

The Last Poem in the Series

The scholar who studies the life of Jesse and Frank
needs solitude.
This person approaches a cabin through fields and
some woods, slowly,
seriously, as if they were going there to take vows.
Everything else
has flown away.

There are no other people.

The flame shapes of cedar and scrub oak are
drawing something huge and
nourishing out of the clay subsoil, a substance we
can only guess at.
Johnson grass burns in its low fires, the color of

prairies. The
sky at this hour and season is a gemmed glass, blue
and refreshing,
it has raised our broken sight many times before
this. In the cabin
are the voices of the original angers. They wait. It
is up to the
person who wants solitude to abandon them. If you
release them they
will fly off like birds or trains. Your skull is very
small under
the awning of the universe. All the time you walk
toward the cabin
huge electrons are raining down on you out of the
heart of the sun.

What do you think of that? Before you can step in
the door, surrender
and disarm. It is a kind of bank, and can be robbed
only by the
anti-bandit.

This is the end of the story of Jesse and Frank.
The grass pours by in the white wind like a river
out of the hill
country, flooding and breaking, and you are
smoothed by its lengthy
currents.

And so you walk in the door of the bank, your
hands are empty.

APPENDIX I

A Jesse James time line,
including principal crimes attributed to the
James-Younger Gang

December 28, 1841

Robert Sallee James and Zerelda Elizabeth Cole, parents of Jesse James, are married at Stamping Ground, Scott County, Kentucky.

January 10, 1843

Alexander Franklin "Frank" James is born at family farm near Centerville (now Kearney), in Clay County, Missouri.

September 5, 1847

Jesse Woodson James is born at the James Farm near Centerville (now Kearney), in Clay County, Missouri.

August 18, 1850

Reverend Robert James, father of Jesse and Frank, dies at a gold camp near Placerville, California.

September 30, 1852

Zerelda James marries Benjamin Simms in Clay County, Missouri.

January 2, 1854

Benjamin Simms is killed in a horse accident in Clinton County, Missouri.

September 25, 1855

Zerelda James Simms marries Dr. Reuben Samuel in Centerville (now Kearney), Clay County, Missouri.

May 4, 1861

Frank James joins the Missouri State Guard. He falls ill at the Battle of Wilson's Creek, is captured, and is eventually paroled.

Summer 1862

Frank James joins William Clarke Quantrill's Confederate guerrillas.

May 1863

Union raid on the James Farm takes place. Jesse James is questioned and horsewhipped. Dr. Samuel is repeatedly hanged from a tree in the yard, but survives.

August 21, 1863

Lawrence Massacre occurs. Frank James is present.

Spring 1864

Jesse James joins the company of William "Bloody Bill" Anderson, who is attached to the command of Guerrilla Chieftain William Clarke Quantrill.

September 27, 1864

Centralia Massacre. Jesse James is said to have killed Union Major A.V. Johnson and possibly seven others.

Summer 1864

Jesse James is severely wounded in Carroll County, Missouri.

October 27, 1864

"Bloody Bill" Anderson is killed in an ambush in Ray County, Missouri, near the old settlement of Albany.

May 1865

Jesse James is seriously wounded on his way to surrender at Lexington, Missouri.

February 13, 1866

The Clay County Savings Bank at Liberty, Missouri, is robbed. Members of the James and Younger families are among the ten to fourteen members of the gang. Approximately $62,000 in cash, specie, and bonds is taken. A young bystander, "Jolly" Wymore, is killed.

October 30, 1866

The Alexander Mitchell & Co. bank in Lexington, Missouri, is robbed. Two thousand to five thousand dollars is taken.

March 2, 1867

At Savannah, Missouri, an attempt is made to rob the Judge John McClain Banking House. McClain is wounded.

May 22, 1867

At Richmond, Missouri, the Hughes and Wasson Bank is robbed. Three townsmen are shot and killed. Approximately $4,000 is taken.

November 27, 1867

At Independence, Missouri, the Stone, McCoy & Co. bank is robbed of $30,000 to $50,000.

March 20, 1868

At Russellville, Kentucky, the Nimrod Long & Co. is robbed. Approximately $12,000 to $14,000 is taken. One bank employee was wounded.

December 7, 1869

At Gallatin, Missouri, the Daviess County Savings Bank is robbed. Cashier John W. Sheets is killed and one other bank employee is wounded. Approximately $1,000 is taken.

June 3, 1871

At Corydon, Iowa, the Ocobock Brothers' Bank is robbed. Approximately $6,000 is taken.

April 29, 1872

At Columbia, Kentucky, the Deposit Bank is robbed. Cashier R. A. C. Martin is killed. Approximately $1,000 is taken.

September 26, 1872

The Kansas City Fairgrounds ticket office is robbed of about $1,000. One young bystander is wounded.

May 27, 1873

At Ste. Genevieve, Missouri, the Ste. Genevieve Savings Bank is robbed of approximately $4,000 to $5,000.

July 21, 1873

Near Adair, Iowa, a Chicago, Rock Island and Pacific Railroad train is derailed and robbed. The engineer, John Rafferty, is killed in the wreck. Approximately $3,000 is taken.

January 15, 1874

At Gulpha Creek, near Hot Springs, Arkansas, the El Paso stagecoach is robbed. Approximately $2,200 in cash and jewelry is taken.

January 31, 1874

Near Gads Hill, Missouri, an Iron Mountain Railway train is robbed. Approximately $5,000 is taken.

March 11, 1874

Pinkerton Detective Agency operative Joseph Whicher is found shot to death near Blue Mills, Missouri.

March 17, 1874

Near Roscoe, in St. Clair County, Missouri, a confrontation between gang members and the Pinkerton Agents results in the death of John Younger. Lewis J. Lull and Edwin B. Daniel, Pinkerton operatives, are also killed.

April 7, 1874

Near Austin, Texas, a stagecoach is robbed. Approximately $3,000 is taken.

April 24, 1874

Jesse James marries Zerelda Amanda "Zee" Mimms at Kearney, Missouri.

June 6, 1874

Frank James marries Anna Ralston.

August 30, 1874

In Carroll County, Missouri, the Waverly-Carrollton omnibus is robbed. At North Lexington, in Ray County, Missouri, another omnibus is robbed the same day.

December 7, 1874

At Corinth, Mississippi, the Tishimingo Savings Bank is robbed of approximately $5,000 to $10,000.

December 8, 1874

At Muncie, Kansas, a Kansas Pacific Railroad train is robbed. An estimated $50,000 was taken.

January 26, 1875

The James Farm home is bombed by agents of the Pinkerton Detective Agency. Young Archie Samuel, the half-brother of Jesse and Frank, is killed and their mother's arm is badly injured and later amputated.

April 12, 1875

Daniel Askew, a neighbor thought to have aided the Pinkerton Detective Agency, is murdered.

August 31, 1875

A son, Jesse Edwards James, is born to Jesse and Zee James at Nashville, Tennessee.

September 5, 1875

The Huntington Bank in Huntington, West Virginia, is robbed of between $10,000 and $20,000. A known gang member, Thompson McDaniel, is killed during escape and Jack Keene is captured.

July 7, 1876

Near Otterville, Missouri, a Missouri Pacific Railroad train is robbed of approximately $15,000. Gang member Hobbs Kerry is later captured. He gives a full confession.

September 7, 1876

At Northfield, Minnesota, an attempt is made to rob the First National Bank of Northfield. Cashier Joseph L. Heywood and a citizen, Nicolas Gustafson, are killed. Gang members Bill Chadwell and Clell Miller are killed in the street.

September 21, 1876

At Hanska Slough, near Madelia, Minnesota, gang members Cole Younger, Jim Younger, and Bob Younger are captured. Another gang member, Charlie Pitts, is killed.

February 6, 1877

A son, Robert Franklin James, is born to Frank and Anna James near Kearney, Clay County, Missouri.

February 28, 1878

Twin sons, Gould and Montgomery James, are born to Jesse and Zee near Box's Station, Nashville, Davidson County, Tennessee. The infants both die within a few days.

June 17, 1879

A daughter, Mary Susan James, is born to Jesse and Zee James at Nashville, Davidson County, Tennessee.

October 8, 1879

Near Glendale Station, in Jackson County, Missouri, a Chicago & Alton Railroad train is robbed of approximately $40,000.

September 3, 1880

Near Mammoth Cave, Kentucky, the Florida stagecoach is robbed. Approximately $2,000 is taken.

March 11, 1881

Near Muscle Shoals, Alabama, approximately $5,200 is taken from a U.S. government paymaster.

July 15, 1881

Near Winston, in Daviess County, Missouri, a Chicago, Rock Island & Pacific Railroad train is robbed. Approximately $2,000 in cash and jewelry is taken. The conductor, William Westfall, and a passenger, Frank McMillan, are killed.

September 7, 1881

At Blue Cut, near Independence, Missouri, a Chicago & Alton Railroad train is robbed. Approximately $3,000 in cash and jewelry is taken.

April 3, 1882

At 1318 Lafayette Street, in St. Joseph, Missouri, Jesse James is assassinated by Robert Ford. Gang member Charles Ford is also present.

April 6, 1882

Jesse Woodson James is buried at the James Farm, near Kearney, Missouri.

April 7, 1882

Robert and Charles Ford plead guilty to the murder of Jesse Woodson James. They are promptly pardoned by Missouri Governor Thomas T. Crittenden.

October 5, 1882

Frank James surrenders to Missouri Governor Thomas T. Crittendon at Jefferson City, Missouri.

January 23, 1883

Charges against Frank James in the murder of Joseph W. Whicher are dismissed.

August 21, 1883

Frank James comes to trial at Gallatin, Missouri, for the murder of Frank McMillan at Winston. He is acquitted.

November 5, 1883

Charges against Frank James for the murder of William Westfall at Winston are dismissed. The case for the murder of John Sheets at Gallatin is continued and eventually dropped.

February 11, 1884

Charges against Frank James for the Blue Cut train robbery are dismissed.

April 17, 1884

Frank James is arraigned at Huntsville, Alabama, for the robbery of Alexander Smith, government paymaster at Muscle Shoals, Alabama. He is found not guilty.

November 13, 1900

Zee James dies at Kansas City, Missouri.

June 29, 1902

Jesse Woodson James's body is exhumed from the yard at the James Farm and moved to Mt. Olivet Cemetery in Kearney, Missouri.

March 1, 1908

Dr. Rueben Samuel, Jesse and Frank's stepfather, dies in St. Joseph, Missouri.

February 10, 1911

Zerelda James Samuel, mother of Jesse and Frank, dies near Oklahoma City, Oklahoma.

February 18, 1915

Frank James dies at the James Farm, near Kearney, Missouri.

July 17, 1995

Jesse James's body is exhumed for DNA testing.

October 28, 1995

Jesse James is reburied in Mt. Olivet Cemetery, Kearney, Missouri.

APPENDIX II

Jesse James as he has appeared in movies and on television

YEAR	TITLE	ACTOR PLAYING JESSE
1908	*The James Boys in Missouri* (silent)	Harry McCabe
1921	*Jesse James under the Black Flag* (silent)	Jesse James, Jr.
1921	*Jesse James as the Outlaw* (silent)	Jesse James, Jr.
1927	*Jesse James*	Fred Thompson
1939	*Days of Jesse James*	Don "Red" Barry
1939	*Jesse James*	Tyrone Power
1940	*The Return of Frank James*	Tyrone Power (stock footage from *Jesse James*)
1941	*Bad Men of Missouri*	Alan Baxter
1941	*Jesse James at Bay*	Roy Rogers
1942	*The Remarkable Andrew*	Rod Cameron
1943	*The Kansan*	George Reeves
1946	*Badman's Territory*	Lawrence Tierney
1947	*Jesse James Rides Again*	Clayton Moore
1948	*Adventures of Frank and Jesse James*	Clayton Moore
1949	*I Shot Jesse James*	Reed Hadley
1949	*The James Brothers of Missouri*	Keith Richards
1949	*Fighting Men of the Plains*	Dale Robertson
1950	*Kansas Raiders*	Audie Murphy
1951	*The Great Missouri Raid*	MacDonald Carey
1951	*Best of the Badmen*	Lawrence Tierney
1953	*The Woman They Almost Lynched*	Ben Cooper

1953	*The Great Jesse James Raid*	Willard Parker (as adult Jesse)
		Tommy Walker (as young Jesse)
1954	*Jesse James' Women*	Don "Red" Barry
1955	*Outlaw Treasure*	Harry Lauter
1957	*Hell's Crossroads*	Henry Brandon
1957	*The True Story of Jesse James*	Robert Wagner
1959	*Alias Jesse James* (Bob Hope comedy)	Wendell Corey
1960	*Young Jesse James*	Ray Stricklyn
1965	*The Outlaws Is Coming* (Three Stooges)	Wayne Mack
1966	*Jesse James Meets Frankenstein's Daughter*	John Lupton
1969	*A Time for Dying*	Audie Murphy
1970	*The Intruders* (TV movie)	Stuart Margolin
1972	*The Great Northfield Minnesota Raid*	Robert Duvall
1977	*Another Man, Another Chance* (France/USA)	Christopher Lloyd
1979	*Last Ride of the Dalton Gang* (TV movie)	Harris Yulin
1980	*The Long Riders*	James Keach
1986	*The Last Days of Frank & Jesse James* (TV movie)	Kris Kristofferson
1990	*Stairway to Paradise*	Jeff James
1994	*Frank & Jesse*	Rob Lowe
1995	*Cyber Vengeance*	Craig Teper
1999	*Purgatory* (TV movie)	J. D. Souther
2001	*American Outlaws*	Colin Farrell
2003	*Outlaws of Missouri*	Bruce McDonald
2007	*The Assassination of Jesse James by the Coward Robert Ford*	Brad Pitt

APPENDIX III

Known and suspected members of the James-Younger Gang

Anderson, James
Armstrong, Frank
Bassham, Daniel "Tuck"
Bishop, Jack
Blackamore, Thomas Jefferson
Bond, Melvin
Book, Aaron
Bradley, Felix G.
Bradley, Newton
Bugler, John
Burns, Richard
Carter, Cal
Chapman, Creed
Chiles, William
Clay, William
Clement, Archibald J. "Archie"
Cooper, Ben
Couch, James C.
Cummins, James Robert "Jim"
Dalton, Kit
Daniels, Edwin
Deardorf, Charles (sometimes spelled Dearduff or Deardolf)
Devers, James M.
Diggs, Andrew Moorman
Easter, William
Edmunson, J. F.
Flannery, Isaac
Ford, Charles
Ford, Robert Newton
Foster, Arnold
Gregg, Frank
Hines, John
Hite, Clarence Browder "Clarence" or "Jeff"
Hite, Robert Woodson "Wood"
Hulse, William
James, Alexander Franklin "Frank"
James, Jesse Woodson

Jarrette, John
Jones, Payne
Judson, Billy
Kerry, Hobbs
Koughman, James
Land, John
Liddil, James Andrew "Dick"
Little, Lorenzo Merrimon
Little, Thomas
Matt, John
McCoy, Arthur C.
McDaniel, Thompson "Tom"
McDaniel, William "Bud"
McGuire, Andrew
McKeehan, Thomas John (AKA Jack Keene, Matt Keene, and T. J. Webb)
Meyers, Fred
Miller, Clelland B. "Clell"
Miller, Edward
Munkers, Redmond B. "Red" *(sometimes spelled Monkers or Monkus)*
Parmer, Allen H.
Pence, Alexander Doniphan "Donnie"
Pence, Thomas E. "Bud"
Perry, Joab
Pitts, Charles (AKA Sam Wells)
Pope, Robert
Purdy, W. E.
Reed, James C. "Jim"
Reed, Solomon Lafe "Sol"
Reynolds, William
Ryan, William
Shepherd, George Washington
Shepherd, Oliver B. "Ol"
Singleton, Bud
Smith, L. S. "Yankee"
Stiles, William *(AKA Bill Chadwell)*
White, James
White, John
Wilkerson, James
Wilkerson, William
Wright, James
Younger, James Henry "Jim"
Younger, John
Younger, Robert Newton "Bob"
Younger, Thomas Coleman "Cole"

PERMISSIONS ACKNOWLEDGMENTS

Strenuous Americans by R. F. Dibble, an excerpt from the chapter entitled, "Jesse James," originally published in 1925 by George Routledge & Sons, LTD, Broadway House: Carter Lane, E. C., London.

Jesse James: My Father by Jesse James, Jr., an excerpt from a chapter entitled, "The James Family." Originally published in 1899 by the Sentinel Printing Co. and reprinted by Triton Press, Provo, Utah, in 1988.

The Life Story of the James and Younger Gang and Their Comrades, Including the Operations of Quantrell's Guerillas by One Who Rode with Them: A True but Terrible Tale of Outlawry, by Jim Cummins, an excerpt from a chapter entitled, "The James Boys—A Little Biography," Originally published in 1903 by the Reed Publishing Company, Denver, Colorado.

Jesse James Was His Name: or, Fact and Fiction Concerning the Careers of the Notorious James Brothers of Missouri, by William A. Settle, Jr., by permission of the University of Missouri Press. Copyright © 1966 by the Curators of the University of Missouri.

Jesse James: Last Rebel of the Civil War by T. J. Stiles, copyright © 2002 by T. J. Stiles. Used by permission of Alfred A. Knopf, a division of Random House, Inc.

"A Terrible Quintette" by John Newman Edwards as published November 22, 1873 by the *St. Louis Dispatch*, St. Louis, Missouri. Edited by Robert Wybrow, 2002.

Rebel Gun by Arthur Steuer, originally published in 1956 by Dell Publishing Co., Inc., New York.

The Jesse James Poems by Paulette Jiles, poems entitled, "Folk Tale," "Jesse Is Thrown Out of the New Hope Baptist Church," and "The Last Poem in the Series." Originally published in 1988 by Polestar Press Ltd., British Columbia, Canada. Reprinted by permission of the author.

Under the Black Flag by Captain Kit Dalton, a Confederate soldier, an excerpt from a chapter entitled, "To Old Mexico, an Unfortunate Affair at a Dance." Originally published 1914 by Lockard Publishing Co., Memphis, Tennessee, and reprinted in 1995 by Larry J. Tolbert.

From JESSE JAMES WAS MY NEIGHBOR by Homer Croy, copyright 1949 by Homer Croy. Used by permission of Dutton, a division of Penguin Group (USA) Inc.

Wanted! by Arthur Winfield Knight, poems entitled, "Jesse James: Robin Hood" and "Zerelda James: At Jesse's Grave." Originally published in 1988 by Trout Creek Press. Reprinted by permission of the author.

Outlaws of the Border: A Complete and Authentic History of the Lives of Frank and Jesse James, the Younger Brothers, and Their Robber Companions, Including Quantrell and His Noted Guerillas, the Greatest Bandits the World Has Ever Known by Jay Donald, an excerpt from the chapter entitled, "Jesse's Courtship and Marriage—a Romantic Story of Love and Danger—a Strange Wedding Tour." Originally published in 1882 by The Coburn & Newman Publishing Company, Chicago, Illinois.

The Life, Times and Treacherous Death of Jesse James by Frank Triplett, an excerpt from chapters entitled, "The Train Robbery at Gads' Hill" and "Whicher's Death." Originally published in 1882 by J. H. Chambers and Co., St. Louis, Missouri.

Speeches and Writings of Wm. H. Wallace by William H. Wallace, originally published in 1914 by The Western Baptist Publishing Co., of Kansas City, Missouri.

Collected Poems by Max Douglas, poems entitled, "The Perils," "Coroner's Inquest Resumed," "The Personal Property of," and "The True Story of the Death of Charlie Ford." Originally published in 1978 by White Dot Press, Washington, D.C. Reprinted by permission of Christopher Weinert, Editor.

Frank and Jesse James: The Story Behind the Legend by Ted P. Yeatman, an excerpt from a chapter entitled, "The Hunters and the Hunted." Copyright © 2000 by Ted P. Yeatman. Reprinted by permission of Cumberland House Publishing, Inc., Nashville, Tennessee.

The Jesse James Northfield Raid: Confessions of the Ninth Man by John Koblas, excerpted from a chapter entitled, "They're Robbing the Bank!" Originally published in 1999 by North Star Press of St. Cloud, Inc., St. Cloud, Minnesota. Reprinted by permission of the publisher.

Ozark Folksongs, Volume II: Songs of the South and West, collected and edited by Vance Randolph, by permission of the University of Missouri Press. Copyright © 1980 by the Curators of the University of Missouri.

Frontier Dust by John Lord, excerpted from a chapter entitled, "The James Boys." Originally published in 1926 by Edwin Valentine Mitchell, Hartford, Connecticut.

A Frontier Doctor by Henry F. Hoyt, excerpted from a chapter entitled, "I Become a Bartender and Eat with Jesse." Originally published in 1928, reprinted in 1979 by R. R. Donnelly & Sons Company, Chicago.

The Romance of a Western Boy: The Story of Corse Payton by Gertrude Andrews, excerpted from a chapter entitled, "A Tragic Night Ride." Originally published in 1901 by The Andrews Press, Brooklyn, New York.

The James Boys: A Thrilling Story of the Adventures and Exploits of Frank and Jesse James by Anonymous, excerpted from a chapter entitled, "The Plot Thickens." Originally published circa 1882, and reprinted in 1947 by Nifty Nut Novelty Co., Excelsior Springs, Missouri.

The Secret Life of Jesse James by Arthur Winfield Knight, an excerpt from a chapter entitled, "1880–1882" Originally published by Burnhill Wolf, Lenoir, North Carolina. Reprinted by permission of the author.

"Good Bye, Jesse!" from the *Kansas City Daily Journal*, April 4, 1882.

Adventures of a Tramp Printer by John Edward Hicks, an excerpt from a chapter entitled, "Death of an Outlaw King." Originally published in 1950 by Midamericana Press, Kansas City, Missouri. Reprinted by permission of George E. Hicks.

John N. Edwards: Biography, Memoirs, Reminiscences and Recollections, compiled by his wife, Jennie Edwards, an excerpt from a chapter entitled, "The Killing of Jesse James." Originally published in 1889 by Jennie Edwards, Kansas City, Missouri.

Singing Rawhide: A Book of Western Ballads by Harold Hersey, originally published in 1926 by the George H. Doran Company, New York.

The Rise and Fall of Jesse James by Robertus Love, an excerpt from a chapter entitled, "The Little White House with the Green Shutters." Originally published by G. P. Putnam and Sons, 1926, reprinted in 1940 by Blue Ribbon Books, New York and in 1990 by the University of Nebraska Press.

"Jesse James as Robin Hood" by Sam Sackett, originally published in 1980 by *MidAmerica Folklore*, Volume VIII, Numbers 1 and 2, Spring-Fall 1980. Permission to reprint granted by Robert Cochran, Editor, *Overland Review* (formerly *MidAmerica Folklore*).

From MISSOURI BITTERSWEET by MacKinlay Kantor, copyright © 1969 by MacKinlay Kantor. Used by permission of Doubleday, a division of Random House, Inc.

Kenneth A. White

ABOUT THE EDITOR

Harold Dellinger is a bookseller, small press publisher and the author of several well-received books on Missouri historical subjects. He is a former parole officer for the city of Kansas City and has long been interested in outlaw and lawman history. He is a board member of the Friends of the James Farm and a member of many other historical groups.